HAMLET AND SAMSON AGONISTES

ESSAYS IN EXPLORATION

HAMLET AND SAMSON AGONISTES

ESSAYS IN EXPLORATION

S. HOMCHAUDHURI

RELIANCE PUBLISHING HOUSE
NEW DELHI

First Published 1992

Published by special arrangements with North-Eastern Hill University Publications"

ISBN : 81-85047-99-5

Published by
Dr. S.K. Bhatia (Life Member ILA & INSA)
for **RELIANCE PUBLISHING HOUSE**
3026/7H, Ranjit Nagar,
New Delhi-110 008 Ph. 5737377/5722605

Composed by
DTP SERVICES & CONSULTANCY (P) LTD.
A-86/3, Ist Floor, Majlis Park, Azadpur,
Delhi-110 033 Ph. 7216733

Printed at

Garg Offset Works Ph.5701008.

To

My Students who help me grow

CONTENTS

ACKNOWLEDGEMENTS

My grateful thanks are due to Professor Iqbal Narain, Vice-Chancellor, NEHU for the personal interest he has shown in my work and for facilitating its publication under the University's co-publishing scheme.

Prof. J.B. Bhattacharjee and his colleagues in the Pubication Department of our University must know that I am much obliged to them for the help received at a critical stage of the publication of this work.

I also recall with affection and gratitude the services of 'Sarju', 'Riti', 'Bok' and 'Berolyne' who took pains to get me the typescript ready.

It is a very special pleasure to acknowledge the emotional support I received from my wife and children.

S. Homchaudhuri

INTRODUCTION

I have brought together in this book a number of essays on *Hamlet* and *Samson Agonistes* in which (with the exception of '*Samson Agonistes* and Greek Tragedy') the common thread of enquiry can be seen in the focusing on and the examination of the central fact of evil having entrenched itself and caused a debasement and desecration of the situation in which the protagonists find themselves at bay and to which they respond with full percipience. In both there is an implied choice, there are temptations offered—temptations such as only a soul in its authenticity can perceive and reject or steer clear of. In each female inconstancy accounts in great measure for the protagonist's revulsion and agony. And in each, like an antiphonal chant, the hero in his entrapment, indulges in repeated bursts of self—flagellation even as he lashes out at the evil he is condemned to fight. Given the common presence of a loathesome evil, Hamlet and Samson illuminate the moral and spiritual physiognomy of the vision of their authors as few creations of art do.

The evil or the pollution which is its work is seen by Hamlet and none else in his world. This pollution has invisibly taken hold of the entire situation, subtly and decisively undermining life—its vitality and growth. The two essays given to an examination of Ophelia's obtuseness and failure of response are informed by this perception. The other two essays on *Hamlet* aim to bring out the protagonist's dour refusal to acquiesce, the unsuspected vitality of his resources, his perceived problems, his spiritual growth and his mode of redeeming himself.

Of the three other essays, the first is addressed exclusively to *Samson Agonistes* while the second takes up the question of Milton's affiliation to the Greek tragic conception and attempts to bring out the exclusively individual temper of *Samson Agonistes* in an extended study where it is examined along with some Greek tragedies. The last essay is a critical comparative survey of *Hamlet* and *Samson Agonistes* seeking to pinpoint some striking affinities in the midst of some obvious divergences. *Hamlet* and *Samson Agonistes* are separated in time by a good deal more than half a century during which English thought and culture underwent profound phases of transition. Much before the rise of Cromwell, the spirit of tragedy had suffered. The visions of Webster, Tourneur and Middleton could no longer recapture that purity of tone which was Shakespeare's. What is of inestimable importance is that Milton, living in an alien age, recovered the lost integrity of the soul and the lost vision of good and evil-lost, that is, to the tragedies between him and Shakespeare and to the 'heroic drama' to follow. The faculty which enables man to see evil with unblinking eyes, see it as a menace to his soul and fight it in its varying appearances—this is what links *Hamlet* and *Samson Agonistes* in spite of each having its irreducibly individual ethos.

THE BELLIGERENT PRINCE

Charles Williams wrote in 1932:

"..... the play has been and is continually presented from Hamlet's point of view. *If, for once, it could be shown us from the king's it might make a difference*. If, in that second scene, the dark and ominous figure poised beside the throne; if that first line breaking out in a suppressed vague hatred, making its *dreadful half-jeer* 'a little more than kin and less than kind'; if the *continual danger* of the enmity which a pretended dementia (Claudius sees through it) is meant to disguise; if that *suppressed savagery* and pretended dementia creating almost a real madness, if the bitter stabbing at Ophelia, his mother and himself-if these things were stressed in their dreadfulness, we might be aware of more danger and less delay. This Hamlet would be quite as much Shakespeare's if less traditionally theatrical. But I think such a production has not yet been given us, and we are therefore still under the effect of Hamlet's own statement about himself. And Hamlet's view is that he is continually delaying, unpacking his heart with words" (italics added).[1]

This perception of 'more danger and less delay' is unfortunately not fully worked out and represents a neglected view-point. For almost throughout the history of Shakespeare Criticism, Hamlet has been seen as a dithering sort of character, more acted upon than acting. He is the person in the play to whom things happen rather than the one who shapes things by the energy of his will and action. He has seldom been accounted a resolute character.

Thus Samuel Johnson says, "Hamlet is, through the whole play, rather an instrument than agent".[2]

In Coleridge's eyes, "Hamlet's character is the prevalence of the abstracting, the generalising habit over the practical".[3] He sees Hamlet's mind "constantly occupied with the world within, and abstracted from the world without-giving substance to shadows and throwing a mist over all commonplace actualities."[4]

For Hazlitt, 'the charcter of Hamlet stands quite by itself. It is not a character marked by strength of will or even of passion but by refinement of thought and sentiment. He is as little of the Hero as a man can well be'.[5]

In our age Eliot sees him making a "pretty considerable mess of things",[6] thus charging him with almost unpardonable remissness.

For Helen Gardner, "the possibility of freedom is the very thing which is in question in Hamlet. The infected will, the dubieties of moral choice, the confusions of speculation are different aspects of our sense of bondage ...... At the close the hero finds death at another's hand, and not by choice."[7]

Critical attention, thus, is generally focused on the time taken by Hamlet in redeeming his pledge to the Ghost and on his soliloquies to the obvious exclusion of the areas in which he shows a remarkable measure of energy and self--assertion in defeating the king's attempts, first to cajole him into accepting the present dispensation, then to ferret out his secret, and then finally to get rid of him physicallly. What is important to realise is that Claudius's sly moves need to be effectually combated even in the process of accomplishing the primary job of revenge.

The object of this essay is to present a reading of Hamlet, which by exploring some critically under-emphasised areas of his behaviour, will seek to project a sharply different image of him. Seen in this light, he probes assiduously, grills with a passion bordering on savagery and defies his enemy whom he sends cowering. In the process he brings into an arresting focus the resources of the Renaissance spirit and emblazons the disconcerting complexity of Renaissance vision.

Hamlet's immediate response to the Ghost's revelation is of an energy and impulse that are reminiscent of Oedipus's intellect and will.

When Creon has returned from the pythian temple carrying Apollo's word that a pollution has to be driven away from the land in the sense that Laius's murderer (no one knows who he is, for the murder has remained wrapped in mystery) has to be identified and banished, Oedipus, tense and resolute, delivers himself thus:

> I will bring this to light again. King Phoebus
> fittingly took this care about the dead,
> and you too fittingly.
> and justly you will see in me an ally,
> a champion of my country and the God.
> For when I drive pollution from the land,
> I will not serve a distant friend's advantage,
> but act in my own interest.
> ....
> Call the assembly
> And let it meet upon the understanding
> That I'll do everything God will decide
> Whether we prosper of remain in sorrow.[8]

To the Ghost's exhortation; 'Hamlet remember me', Hamlet replies:

> Remember thee!
> Yea, from the table of my memory
> I'll wipe away all trivial fond records,
> ....
> And thy commandment all alone shall live
> Unmix'd with baser matter.

Hamlet's response is on all fours with Oedipus's, although the mode of action he chooses is different from that of Oedipus, for the situation is different. He has to act warily. He is under surveillance.

However, his dealings with those who gratuitously or under command throw themselves in his way have a masterful decisiveness indicating his being the master of the situation (witness what he does to Polonius, the two old pals now turned spies, and the pirates).

Even before these exploits, the manner of his meeting the Ghost in the face of his friends stubbornly seeking to dissuade him from his course clean sets him apart from the commonalty. And, then, after he has taken leave of the Ghost, his manner of going about arming himself with an inflexible purpose, and taking Horatio and Marcellus into his confidence, while not giving himself away is no mean evidence that he has, indeed, a mind of his own and, besides, that the can shape things to his own end.

And if we look back for a while, we can meet the bereaved prince, who is to appear much later in a scene with the exultingly defiant cry 'Here I am, Hamlet the Dane', jeering savagely (although in an undertone) in his 'inky cloak', holding his own, though with a touch of melancholy, and in the process hinting at something inside him which 'passeth show'. He agrees to obey his majesty, but not before he has had his distinctive temper etched inerasively on the mind of the audience. This easily remarkable first encounter with Hamlet is a foreshadowing of those future glimpses, not as infrequent as is commonly made out, of an unusual prince who is no stranger to the concept or world of action as we shall seek to understand it.

His gift of imaginative thinking which often sets him on edge hardly saps his will. At the sight of that ominous apparition, when others shrink and cower (and they are soldiers), the prince shows an unflappability of bearing which astonishes and disconcerts the onlookers almost as much as does the apparition itself.

It is worth recalling that leaving aside his clowns and fools who are ever at it, Hamlet, as no other character in Shakespeare, is seen so habitually quibbling and punning-a distinctively Elizabethan turn of mind.

Now this punning can be seen to be both a natural and a consciously chosen idiom of the man enmeshed in a situation in the creation of which he had no hand. Here, in a way, lies the uniqueness of the play. In neither *Othello*, nor *Macbeth*, nor *King Lear* is there a desperate situation at the outset not in any way brought into being by the hero.

It is a world of evil-a world of murder and incest-which exists independently of Hamlet's choice and action. It is a fact presented to his consciousness which is continually and increasingly tortured and inflamed by it. In both *Macbeth* and *Lear* evil results from the hero's action. In Othello evil is no doubt already there in the person of Iago, but its destructive potential would not break out into open fury if Othello knew better than he did. Othello is the reason why lago succeeds. Hamlet is not the reason why Claudius succeeds in murdering his father and seducing and marrying his mother. Both the things happen and he was an outsider and now he is a trapped insider.

With all natural ties treacherously snapped and his ardent youthful impulse to forge a tie with Ophelia thwarted, Hamlet suffers from a sense of total outrage. There is only Horatio to whom he can unburden himself and whose counsel he can seek. Waking up in a world in which he finds his reason and will not only of no account, but frightfully meant to subserve the joint will of the murderer and the adulteress he grows claustrophobic. For him it is an unspeakably oppressive and tyrannical at mosphere bearing down upon him. There is no fresh air to breathe. The air smells of pollution.

He is not meant to think or act freely. For he is not a free individual. The present is none of his choice. Indeed, it is forced, clamped upon him and he is meant to fit into it. The future, whatever it be, can only grow out of the present. And he must make no protest. Not only that he should get reconciled to it, but he should accept the present dispensation with cheer and a smile.

For Claudius Hamlet should be no better than a caged animal that dances to his tune and brings him pleasure. Here, then, is the greatest affront to the Renaissance prince who prizes his freedom of choice as issuing inevitably from his most cherished concept of the inviolability of reason and its unrestricted play. But think and act he must. And he needs time in which to make sure of things.

II

The serpent as a literary image has the weight of a whole tradition behind it. The serpent was the subtlest of God's creatures in Eden and caused incalculable damage to the human pair. It stands for guile and a frightening destructive potential. It undermines order, 'degree' by covert means. It has fell designs and a glozing tongue. It is the archetypal subverter. It is the archetypal forger of meretricious lies.

> "And the great dragon was cast out, that old serpent, called the Devil, and Satan, which deceiveth the whole world: he was cast out into the earth and his angels were cast out with him".
>
> Revelation 12:9

The Ghost's references to Claudius exploit the traditional conception of the Devil in full richness of detail. Its cunning and deceit, its glibness, its lasciviousness- all this is overtly suggested:

> Ah, that incestuous, that adulterate, beast,
> With witchcraft of his wit, with traitorous gifts,-
> O wicked wit, and gifts that have the power
> So to seduce-won to his shameful lust
> The will of my most seeming virtuous queen:

The Ghost talks of Claudius's lewdness courting Gertrude "in a shape of heaven". The royal bed of Denmark has become "a couch for luxury and damned incest". Marlowe's dramatisation of the Devil possessing Faustus's soul readily comes to mind: Faustus is depicted as savouring the sight of the Seven Deadly Sins. His lasciviousness is continually emphasised. Milton's epic realisation of the vice of lechery in all its hideousness can perhaps be equally pertinently recalled here:

> Belial came last, than whom a spirit more lewd Fell not from Heaven, or more gross to love Vice for itself.
>
> .... who filled
> With lust and violence the house of God?
> In courts and palaces he also reigns,
> And in luxurious cities.......(Paradise Lost BK I)
>
> On the other side up rose
> Belial, in act more graceful and humane,
> A fairer person lost not Heaven;
> For dignity composed, and high exploit.

But all was false and hollow; thought his tongue
Dropped Manna, and could make the worse appear
The better reason, to perplex and dash
Maturest counsels: for his thoughts were law
To vice industrious, but to nobler deeds
Timorous and slothful. Yet he pleased the ear,
And with persuasive accent thus began; (P.L.BK II)

In the person of Claudius is realised the hoary tradition of evil seeking to possess the soul of mankind here represented by Hamlet. The plausibility of evil has been the greatest snare for man. Claudius' plausibility is indeed decisive for the unwary and grimly distrubing for the discerning mind. By reason of the 'witchcraft of wit', the evil has already made a conquest of the world-a conquest which it is now seeking to consolidate and extend. Hamlet is the only refractory element which has to be subdued and brought to subjection. The alien recalcitrance of Hamlet has to be conquered. And to this effect it employs all the plenary resources of its wit.

Hamlet scents the approach and closing in of evil and the forces in its pay. The King's opening speech is a master-piece of rhetorical virtuosity designed with the utmost deliberation to conceal his real self and project the image of a judicious, public-spirited ruler who has had to battle with his conscience to mute the anguish and cry of bereavement in the interest of state affairs which must be given precedence over private grief.

Polonius, to prove his indispensability to the King, whose mind misgives on account of Hamlet's 'transformation', takes it upon himself gratuitously to play the eaves-dropper when the prince is closeted with Ophelia or Gertrude. He has already proferred his services to elicit the cause of Hamlet's distemper.

Rosencrantz and Guildenstern have been commissioned to ply Hamlet with a view to fishing out his secret. The evil is triumphant, for it has won acceptance by an unsuspecting world; in fact, it has been emboldened by the genuflection it has received. Nevertheless, it is not complacent, it is wary. Its agents are up and about. Hamlet is encircled, hemmed in.

What does he do thus seeing himself imperilled? What he does constitutes a peremptory, yet artful gesture of his beleagured self. If Claudius can muster his rhetoric and further ensure that Hamlet is watched and spied upon, should Hamlet just cave in? Or, should he not attempt to hoist Claudius with his own petard? Rooted in and nourished at once be the popular and classical traditions, a Renaissance prince has his own

This is an excellent specimen of Elizabethan punning—especially the kind of punning that we associate with Shakespearean fools. It derives from the long tradition of verbal acrobatics, of getting the most out of words in a witty combat - a keen attitude of mind and a zestful habit that had received a peculiar impetus from the sustained and wide-spread training in logic and rhetoric as part of Renaissance culture. It speaks of the zest (that had gradually cut across the barrier of classes) for the racy tang and the salty savour of a debate where no holds are barred. Demonstrating a kind of verbal pugilism Hamlet tells his erst-while friends where they now truly belong - the slimy world of moral promiscuity, thus putting them in their place. The traditional medieval image of fortune as an inconstant woman now smiling and now frowning and promiscuously bestowing favours is made the most of in an argument that calls attention to the very heart of the play.

There are surprises almost at every step for them as the prince goes about ruthlessly establishing his view of things and tearing to shreds the logic of his opponents:

Ham : ....Let me question more in particular : What have you, my good friends, deserved at the hands of fortune, that she sends you to prison hither?

Guil : Prison, my Lord?

Ham : Denmark is a prison.

Ros : Then is the world one.

Ham : A goodly one; in which there are many confines, wards and dungeons, Denmark being one o' the worst.

Ros : Why, then, your ambition makes it one; 'tis too narrow for your mind.

Ham : O God. I could be bounded in a nut-shell and count myself a King of infinite space were it not that I have had bad dreams.

Guil : Which dreams, indeed, are ambition; for the very substance of the ambitious is merely the shadow of a dream.

Ham : A dream itself is but a shadow.

Ros : Truly, and I hold ambition of so airy and light a quality that it is but a shadow's shadow.

Ham : Then are our beggars bodies and our monarchs and outs tretched heroes the beggars' shadows, Shall we to the court? For, by my fay, I cannot reason.

We know he has reasoned to some effect for his opponents' quivers are now left empty. By a dexterous turn of logic he has pointed the absurdity and hollowness of their propositions and the poverty of their wit. He shows how spurious their logic is. Indeed, they are the agents of a spurious authority.

He lets them know that he is alive to being "most dreadfully attended".

Hamlet then has clean got the better of the spies and they see no way but to confess to their mission:

Guil : My Lord, we were sent for.

With savage sarcasm and withering scorn Hamlet tells his pursuers what they are worth, what he thinks of them, and how, no matter how keen the thrust of their endeavour, he can keep his counsel:

Hamlet : Why do you go about to recover the wind of me, as if you would drive me into a toil?

Guil : O, my Lord, if my duty be too bold my love is too unmannerly.

Ham : I do not understand that. Will you play upon this pipe?

Guil : My Lord, I cannot.

Ham : I pray you.

Guil : Believe me, I cannot.

Ham : I do beseech you.

Guil : I know no touch of it, my Lord.

Ham : Tis as easy as lying govern these ventages with your finger thumb, give it breath with your mouth, and it will discourse most eloquent music. Look you, these are the stops.

Guil : But these I connot command to any utterance of harmony : I have not the skill.

Ham: Why, look you now, how unworthy a thing you make of me. You would play upon me; you would seem to know my stops; you would pluck out the heart of my mystery; you would sound me from the lowest note to the top of my compass : and there is much music, excellent voice in this little organ; yet cannot you make it speak. S' blood do you think that I am easier to be played on than a pipe? Call me what instrument you will, though you can fret me you cannot play upon me.

Hamlet breathes menace and the spying mission fails of its object. From their next employment by the King Hamlet's erstwhile friends have no means of returning at all while Hamlet, the intended victim, returns to Claudius's amazement and disbelief.

We have seen Samuel Johnson describing Hamlet as more an instrument than an agent. But this instrument ('call me what instrument you will') has a mind of its own and renders futile the hectic plottings of the critically acclaimed doers and agents. Hamlet can be fretted but not played upon. We shall see how Hamlet can both 'fret' Claudius and 'play upon' him. In the meantime he has foiled the latter's attempts to emasculate him, as it were, through the spies.

How does he go about with Polonius, the professed know-all? He has just now suggested a strategem whereby he will convince their majesties that his discovery about Hamlet is true. As they converse, Hamlet appears. Here, feels Polonius, is an opportunity for him to prove his worth. He beseeches them to leave him alone. He will face the youngman and ply him with such cunning and decisiveness as to have his discovery confirmed. Then, presumably, he will run back to his master and report his triumph. How long could this young man hold his secret from the sage and crafty counsellor? He has already told the King that should he be proved wrong,

Let me be no assistant for a state
But keep farm and carters.

Thus with a bursting sense of self-importance he launches his attack, as it were. Mark his words : 'I'll board him presently : O, give me leave', Shakespeare the inimitable ironist is at work. As ever, he is going to show pomposity duly deflated, but not without providing a delectable treat for his audience.

Pol : Do you know me, my Lord?
Ham : Excellent, excellent well; you're a fish monger.
Pol : Not I, my Lord.
Ham : Then I would you were so honest a man.
Pol : Honest, my Lord!
Hm : Ay, Sir, to be honest, as this world goes, is to be one picked out of ten thousand.
Pol : That's very true, my Lord.
Ham : For if the sun breed maggots in a dead dog, being a god-kissing carrion, - Have you a daughter?
Pol : I have, my Lord?
Ham : Let her not walk i' the Sun : conception is a blessing; but not as your daughter may conceive : friend, look to't.

Hamlet proves too subtle and wayward for Polonius who, however, feels he can read some meaning in a phrase or two and puts the rest down to the dissolution of Hamlet's mind. In addition to baffling Polonius, Hamlet has the satisfaction of having given vent to his latelyengendered cynicism, his mistrust of integrity and sex in the putrid atmosphere in which he is so painfully entangled.

Polonius hears Hamlet further on and, struck by a sudden sally which he happens to make sense of, utters the following aside :

'How pregnant sometimes his replies are, a happiness that often madness hits on, which reason and sanity could not so prosperously be delivered of'.

Polonius's startled reaction has a certain family resemblance to the delighted exclamation of Jaques on hearing Touchstone:

'Is not this a rare fellow, my Lord? he's as good as anything, and yet a fool'.

A.Y.L.I. (V.iv).

Finding himself out of his depth, Polonius attempts a retreat: More honourable Lord I will most humbly take my leave'. Indeed, he has been most properly humbled. But he cannot go before he has been duly rated.

'You cannot, Sir, take from me anything that I will more willingly part withal.....'

When Polonius finally takes leave of him Hamlet takes it as a good riddance:

These tedious old fools!

One recalls Touchstone's unflattering opinion of Corin:

> 'Will thou rest damned? God help Thee, shallow man. God make incision in thee! thou art raw. A.Y.L.I. III.ii.

In Act III Sc.II Polonius wearies Hamlet by his slimy obsequiousness and in Sc.IV this busybody of an eavesdropper, after self-importantly instructing the queen to put her son in his place, goes to hide behind the arras never to return from there.

Hamlet's encounter with the King in Act IV Sc. III shows him at his deadly and devastating best. His involved punning on eating, worms and fish carried on and brought to a pulverising end with ferocious pugnacity at once baffles and outrages Claudius who, when Hamlet's fury has abated, tells him of the decision, already taken, to send him to England 'for thine especial safety'. Let us see how Hamlet fires his salvoes. Where's Polonius? Asks Claudius. He is at supper, quips Hamlet, not where he eats, but where he is eaten. With breath taking audacity, he makes a mockery of the dead man who had been the questioner's counsellor-lackey.

> ".....a certain convocation of politic worms are even at him. Your worm is your only emperor for diet. We fat all creatures else to fat us, and we fat our selves for maggots: your fat King and lean beggar is but variable service - two dishes, but to one table: that's the end".
>
> (IV. iii)

With a weird, irrepressible glee Hamlet has already pushed him down to the unenviable level of the beggar and enacted in words the macabre and ego-shattering Dance of Death the Elizabethan audence knew so well. The idea of Death the great leveller that made no distinctions - such as were grossly practised in the corrupted world of medieval and Renaissance civility inwhich thrived all the Seven Deadly Sins and in which God's scheme of justice and equity was set at naught - had a special meaning and appeal (in terms of ultimate compensation) for play-goers.

A second time the King asks - Where is Polonius? and Hamlet quips:

> In heaven; send thither to see if your messenger find him no not there, seek him i' the other place yourself. But, indeed, if you find him not within this month, you shall nose him as you go up the stairs into the lobby.

When the King feigns good will and assures him that the decision to send him to England is for his own good, 'if thou knew'st our purposes', Hamlet's reply is: 'I see a cherub that sees them'. He is as though seized by a demon to tear away all pretences. His satiric zest knows no end. The exiled Duke in *As You Like It* would exclaim:

> He uses his folly like a stalking-horse, and under the presentation of that he shoot his wit. A.Y.L.I.V.Iv

Claudius stands denuded, for he is stripped of all claim to self-respect. And to cap it all, Hamlet has thrown a dark hint in the meshes of his quibbling.

The play within the play is a huge, deadly, practical joke pulled off to Claudius's discomfiture. This is Hamlet's capital achievement in his assumed role. The play is about to begin when he breaks off his conversation with Horatio: 'They are coming to the play; I must be idle'. Both will be watching for the King's reaction during the play at the end of which they will compare notes. Hamlet must now take leave of his normal behaviour to assume the role of the lunatic. And immediately he goes for his satiric digs at both the King and his counsellor.

King : How fares our cousin, Hamlet?

Hamlet : Excellent, i' faith; of the Chameleon's dish: I eat the air, promise-crammed: You cannot feed capons so.

Hamlet thus obliquely reminds the King of his assurance that he was upper-most in his thoughts as being the most immediate to the throne.

But the promise seems as thin and insubstantial as the air on which the chameleon feeds. It is both temerity and misdirection which he can and does resort to under the immunities he enjoys.

With studied deliberation Hamlet keeps harping on his generally believed weakness for Ophelia, occasioning Polonius's rather expected self-congratulatory interjection to the King. With equal deliberation he breaks into a spell of obscenity with Ophelia creating the impression that this is all an expression of a frustrated lover gone mad. With noticeable aplomb and vitality he persists in having digs at the people around him. And now he takes on his mother.

Oph: You are merry, my Lord.

Ham: Who, I?

Oph; Ay, my Lord.

Ham: O, your only jig-maker. What should a man do but he merry? For look you, how cheerfully my mother looks, and my father died within's two hours.

Oph: Nay 'tis twice two months, my Lord.

Ham: So Long? ..... then there's hope a great man's memory may outlive
his life half a year......

At the point where the player - queen protests undying fidelity to the player King:

Both here and hence, pursue me lasting strife.
If, once a widow, ever I be wife!

Hamlet, to feel her pulse, asks Gertrude how she finds the play:

Ger: The lady protests too much, me-thinks.
Ham: O, but she'll keep her word.

Both ~Gertrude's uneasy conscience and Hamlet's ironic quip are worth noting.

Suddenly getting dubious Claudius asks Hamlet if there was no offence in the 'argument' whereupon the latter replies that there is none: 'No, no, they do but jest, poison in jest, no offence i' the world'. Then elaborating the content of the play Hamlet assures him:

".....your majesty, and we that have free souls, it touches
us not: let the galled jade wince, our withers are unwrung."

His barbed speech recalls Jaques' submission to the exiled Duke that his railing at the vices of the world would not touch one who is free from them:

......if he be free,
why, then, my taxing life a wild-goose klies
unclaim'd of any man.

A.Y.L.I. II,vii

This is one of the arresting moments of the play. Hamlet has the royal criminal awkwardly caught in the meshes of his wit. He is quiveringly expectant with the anticipation of discovery. And, then, indeed, the King gives himself away. We hear the triumphant Hamlet: 'O good Horatio, I'll take the ghost's word for a thousand pound'.

Much of the closet scene is a testimony to Hamlet's power of employing wit and invective to masterly effect. One cannot fail to notice the exulting cry with which, so to speak, he jumps into the fray. He was summoned to be given a set-down. Polonius who is soon to pay for his 'pranks' with his very life, has just now advised Gertrude to be 'round with him (Hamlet)'. But who is going to be round with whom? With a kind of wild animation Hamlet enters and no sooner does he enter her chamber and face Gertrude than he looks agression itself, setting his mordant, cutting wit against hers and subjecting her to pitiless exposure. The projected roles get instantly reversed. Gertrude finds herself affronted,.scandalised, terrified. Hamlet is in full cry. Let us hear the dialogue:

Ham : Now, mother, what's the matter?
Queen : Hamlet, thou hast thy father much offended.
Ham : Mother, you have my father much offended.
Queen : Come, come, you answer with an idle tongue.
Ham : Go, go, you question with a wicked tongue.
Queen : Why, how now, Hamlet!
Ham : What's the matter now?
Queen : Have you forgot me?
Ham : No, by the rood, not so:
You are the queen, your husband' brother's wife,
and - would it were not so - you are my mother.

When the queen makes a minatory noise, Hamlet answers with absolute peremptoriness.

Come, come, and sit you down, you shall not budge:
You go not till I set you up a glass
Where you may see the inmost part of you.

The queen panics and raises and alarm, Polonius gets slain. When she calls her son's attention to the 'rash and bloody deed', he jibes savagely and with a sneer:

A bloody deed! - almost as bad, good mother,
As kill a king and marry with his brother.

Gertrude cannot be sure that her son is quite in his senses and that he is not seized with a bout of insanity. In fact, her panicked cry:

'What will thou do? thou will not murder me?
Help, help, ho.

is an expression of fear that Hamlet, in his 'ecstasy', might turn so violent as to take her life. In the face of Hamlet's settled resolve to act the inquisitor: 'And let me wring your heart; for so I shall' the queen cries out:

What have I done that thou dar'st wag thy tongue
In noise so rude against me?

And again when Hamlet hysterically charges her with an act that 'blurs the grace and blush of modesty', her outraged being cries out

Ah me, what act,
That roars so Loud, and thunders in the index?

The most dramatic thing that Hamlet as a frenzied inquisitor does is to present contrasted pictures of his father and uncle and thereby to illumine the very heart of the tragedy. These pictures juxtapose the glory that has passed away from the earth and the depravity and disease that has taken it place. In facing up to the time that is out of joint, that is, the dark deeds of a degenerate humanity, he looks upon himself as heaven's 'scourge and minister'. It is in this role which he has arrogated to himself that he speaks to his mother as to a desecrator, a secrileger. She has made a mockery of everything that was touched with the divine - 'modesty', 'virtue', innocent love', 'marriage-vows'. She has reduced religion to a mere rhapsody of words:

......heaven's face doth glow;
Yes, this solidity and compound mass,
With tristful visage, as against the doom
It thought-sick at the act.

It is in this context that he focuses on the contrast between the dead king and the usurper. The former is spoken of in terms of the images of grace and beauty, power and majesty - images that betoken the high gods. He was

A combination and a form, indeed,
Where every god did seem to set his seal,
To give the world assurance of a man.

Here was a King who was beloved of the gods whom he constantly suggested in his action and bearing. And the present King? He is

'like a mildew'd ear
Blasting his wholesome brother'.

He is a disease, a poisonous growth of life, disfiguring it. The dead King was a 'fair mountain' suggesting beauty and elevation and majesty. The present one is a moor, low and unwholesome, with its overhanging miasma. He is a devil (what devil was't/that thus hath cozen'd you at hoodman-blind?). He is a 'murderer' and a 'villain', a 'slave', a vice of Kings', a 'cut-purse of the empire' (the last phrase strongly suggesting Satan - the potential cut-purse of the celestial empire). A foul contagion has blotted out an era of health and radiance. The resplendent Renaissance ideal of yesterday has plumetted to abysmal depths (note the apt metaphoric transition from mountain to moor).

In his first soliloquy in Act I Sc. II Hamlet had spoken of the two in somewhat similar terms:

> So excellent a King: that was, to this,
> Hyperion to a satyr.

From the blazing sun-god bestriding the heavens to the diminutive, ugly-looking and lecherous wood-god represented partly as a goat - that is the metaphoric equivalent of man's fall from light to darkness, from beauty to ugliness.

It is not without significance that Hamlet is spelling out in greater detail and in more imaginative terms the study in contrast that had been initiated by the Ghost thus:

> O Hamlet, what a falling-off was there!
> From me whose love was of that dignity
> That it went hand in hand even with the vow
> I made to her in marriage: and to decline
> Upon a wretch........
> But virtue, as it never will be mov'd
> Though lewdness court it in a shape of heaven;
> So lust, lthough to a radiant angel link'd, Will
> Will sate itself in a celestial bed
> And prey on garbage.

The decline from 'virtue' to 'lewdness' and from 'a celestial bed' to garbage' is symptomatic of the travesty and collapse of values, of the deceit and depravity of the present. 'Frailty, thy name is woman'. But reason is frail too. Shakespeare dramatises this frailty of reason positing a full and tearing consciousness of it in Hamlet's psyche. Hence, he grieves and storms. Hence, his 'eternal tempest never to be calmed'.

The Renaissance had apotheosized reason, the divine faculty of man aspiring heaven-high and keeping passion in subjection. It had always been alive to the tension bred by the opposition within man of reason and the appetites or passion. At the same time, however, it had come to hope that reason with its heaven-scanning ambition, the guarantee of man's greatness, would be an insurance against the almost inevitable propensity, consequent upon Original Sin, towards depravity and degene ration. That this hope or belief was illusory is proved by the crisis of the times. The precarious grip of reason over passion is the theme of lament and protest. More truly, the fact of reason abdicating its authority and prostituting itself so far as to lose its identity in order to serve the ends of passion is the burden of Hamlet's denunciation. Thus in his horror-struck eyes, 'reason panders will' and Gertrude lives

> In the rank sweet of an enseamed bed
> Stew'd in corruption, honeying and making love
> Over the nasty sty.

Man is a unique creation in a largely foreign world of mere organic vitality. His pre-eminence and glory is because of his being non-animal and non-mechanical. Hamlet has in mind "the scheme of the ideal internal psychic hierarchy in which man's will is liberated from mechanism and released for its glorious work of choice and command"[9]. This non-animal and non-mechanical but inalienably human function of choice and command is dwelt upon by Hamlet as something that even madness could not eclipse and as his most dearly held belief, now shaken by Gertrude's conduct:

> Sense, sure, you have,
> Else could you not have motion, but sure that sense
> Is apoplex'd; for madness would not err;
> Nor sense to ecstasy was ne'er so thrall'd
> But it reserv'd some quantity of choice
> To serve in such a difference.

The 'blood' and 'judgement' satiric thrust that had just preceded the above passage derives from the same mode of thought and is thus seen to fall in place

> Ha! have you eyes?
> You cannot call it love; for at your age
> The hey-day in the blood is tame, it's humble,
> And waits upon the judgement; and what judgement
> Would step from this to this?

If Macbeth's deed reverberates through heaven and hell and Lear's madness embraces an inner and outer storm, Gertrude's act which has struck at the very root of Hamlet's faith affects the universe no less potently and is no less an outrage:

.....heaven's face doth glow;
Yes, this solidity and compound mass,
With tristful visage, as against the doom
Is thought-sick at the act.

This is so because in the great chain of being man occupies a pivotal position and his individual actions find their implications echoed in macrocosmic nature. It is a characteristic Renaissance way of looking at and understanding the inter-related scheme of things. "Levels of existence, including human and cosmic, were habitually correlated and correspondence and resemblances were perceived everywhere. Man as a microcosmic model was thus a mediator between himself and the universe".[10]

Indeed, in what we encounter in the closet scene Hamlet is very much a mediator between himself and the universe; he is the outraged spokesman of Renaissance humanism.

Towards the end of the scene Hamlet mentions to his mother like one mentioning something of moment he was about to forget that he is going to be sent off to England, the dark motive behind which has not altogether eluded his misgiving mind. The important thing for our present purpose is that the manner in which Hamlet talks about the disguised threat to his life and his confidence in his ability not only to frustrate the designs of his opponent but to destroy him at his own game suggest an extraordinary, yet easy superiority of bearing even in the state of contemplating the mortal peril:

Let it work;
For 'tis the sport to have the engineer
Hoist with his own petard: and 't shall go hard.
But I will delve one yard below their mines,
And blow them at the moon.

He is not unnerved, he is zestful. And he seems to be chuckling, even in anticipation, over out-manouevring his enemy. And we know that this is no empty boast, but that he does at the proper moment carry out his grim resolve to outwit his enemy as he himself relates the episode to Horatio in Act V Sc.II. This is certainly not the picture of one who is more an instrument than an agent. The quality of his mind, and, more importantly, his actions are oddly at variance with our notion of someone acting as a mere instrument without a driving passion and will.Unless we see Shakespeare as having designed Hamlet as a doer, as a self propelled agent endowd with a noticeable measure of passion and initiative, we cannot understand how the latter causes the kind of desperation in Claudius's mind finding such expression as the following:

> His liberty is full of threats to all;
> To you yourself, to us, to every one.
> Alas, how shall this bloody deep be answer'd?
> It will be laid to us, whose providence
> should have kept short, restrain'd and out of haunt
> This mad young man.
>
> IV.i
>
> My soul is full of discord and dismay.
>
> IV.i
>
> How dangerous is it that this man goes loose!
>
> VI.iii
>
> I like him not; nor stands it safe with us
> To let his madness range....
> The terms of our estate may not endure
> Hazard so dangerous as doth hourly grow
> Out of his lunacies.
>
> III. iii
>
> Do it, England;
> For like the hectic in my blood he rages
> And thou must cure: till I know 'tis done,
> How'er my haps, my joys will ne'er begin.
>
> IV.iii

And had his author conceived and designed Hamlet as a mere instrument without that cutting decisiveness of will and passion, he would not have been able to rouse Gertrude to an awareness of the blackness of her deed and to win from her the promise not to disclose his secret.

The quality of mind defined by D.H. Lawrence in a letter to Lady Cynthia is the quality that Shakespeare gave Hamlet as the one irreducible mark of his being:

> "One should stick by one's soul; and by nothing else. In one's soul one knows the truth from the untruth, and life from death.

> And if one betrays one's soul-knowledge one is the worst of traitors. I am out of all patience with the submitting to the things that be, however foul they are, just because they happen to be".[11]

Hamlet's decisive refusal to come to terms with evil and betray his soul-knowledge demonstrates how he sticks by his soul and will not be a traitor to himself. Even when caught in the toil of speculations (witness his soliloquies) which would never be resolved to calm his unquiet self, his concern for the inviolability of his soul is over-ridingly stressed. In Hamlet's stark refusal to "commit the vast wickedness of acquiescence"[12] Shakespeare defines not only the physiognomy of his protagonist's soul but also that of the evil he faces. And in the process he illuminates, in unique dramatic terms, the everrecurring predicament of man on this earth and the imperative need for a clear-eyed choice to give battle to the forces of darkness and death.

Thus, in spite of the impression (too often dwelt upon exclusively) of nervelessness and vacillation created by the soliloquies which are too full of selfreproach, Shakespeare does present Hamlet as one implacable in resisting and battling against the evil he sees with such discernment. As we have argued above, Shakespeare's projection of Hamlet seems centred in an unerring recognition of a pollution and a threat and in an artful but masterly resort to a series of actions calculated to arrest the pollution and meet the threat with adequacy.

Of the admittedly various impressions the play yields of the central character, one is undoubtedly, as we have tried to show, that of a person who, in the face of an enormous evil bent on conquest or destruction, opposes his roused and bristling self to its devious and deadly proceedings. It was left for Milton to dramatise a similar crisis of being and a similar refusal to come to terms in *Samson Agonistes* in more distinctively Christian terms.

References:-

1. 'Troilus and Cressida' and 'Hamlet' in *Shakespeare Criticism* 1919-35, ed. Anne Ridler, 1956, pp. 201-22.
2. *Shakespeare Criticism* (1623-1840) ed. Nichol Smith (O.U.P), 1958 p.12
3. Ibid. p. 262.
4. Ibid. pp. 256-57.
5. Ibid. pp. 289.
6. 'Shakespeare and the Stoicism of Seneca' in Shakespeare Criticism 1919-1935, ed. Anne Ridler (O.U.P.) (World's Classics), 1958, p.216.

7. 'The Noble Moor' *in Shakespeare Criticism* (1935-60) ed. Anne Ridler, p. 353.
8. Oedipus the King, trans. David Grene, *Greek Tragedy* - Vol.I, The University of Chicago Press, Phoenix Books.
9. *The Rhetorical World of Augustan Humanism,* p. Fussell, 1967, p.13.
10. 'Shakespeare and the Thought of His Age' in *A New Companion to Shakespeare Studies,* ed. K. Muir and S. Schoenbaum, paper back, 197, p.181.
11. *Selected Letters,* D.H. Lawrence, ed. Richard Aldington,Penguin Books, 198, p.115.
12. Ibid. p.88.

A PASSAGE TO 'HIGHER' REASON—A STUDY OF THE PROBLEM OF HAMLET'S DELAY

'...in action, how like an angel! in apprehension, how like a god'.
(Hamlet. II.ii.)

...whence the Soul
Reason receives, and Reason is her being,
Discursive, or Intuitive: Discourse
Is oftest yours, the latter most is ours,
Differing but in degree, of kind the same.
Time may come when men
With Angels may participate, ...
(*Paradise Lost*, BK. V, 486-94)

II

One can see in *Hamlet* that the possibility of action getting delayed or not taking place at all seems to trouble not only Hamlet but also Claudius and Laertes. The problem of Hamlet's delay, however, is the most conspicuous aspect of the general motif of delay that one sees woven into the design of the Hamlet world. For a proper understanding, therefore, the hero's delay needs to be set in the wider perspective involving a disturbing and quite pervasive awareness of a phenomenon which seems to prevent or delay action.

Claudius for whom Hamlet is a thorn in the flesh has bent all his energies to getting the prince out of his way. But neither Polonius nor Rosencrantz and Guildenstern have been able to be of any help to the king in that direction. Hamlet, in the meanwhile, continues to rob Claudius of his peace. He not only gets staged the impudent Gonzago play but also disposes of Polonius, however unintentionally. Ophelia goes mad. Laertes returns from France and vows like a maniac to avenge his father (who was buried almost on the sly), no matter whoever may have killed the letter. And Hamlet comes back to the bewilderment and fright of Claudius, without ever reaching England where he should have been put to death.

The point in this short recital is that even though Claudius has been going about determinedly trying to find ways to take care of the threat that Hamlet is, his moves have proved infructuous. The dual fact that so agonisingly stares him in the face is that Hamlet very much remains a threat, even adding to his potential for 'mischief' and that more time has elapsed than should have for Claudius in taking decisive action.

To go back a little, he laments to Gertrude that while considerations of safety, both private and public, should long have warranted imposition of physical restraints on Hamlet, "so much was our love" that he stopped short of resorting to that painful course. He has per force had to delay action. (IV.i.19-23)

Following the setback as a result of Hamlet's murder of Polonius, he decides to pack the prince off to England under the escort of Rosencrantz and Guildenstern who will be carrying the royal commission. Made desperate with the growing realisation that he has been remiss in curbing Hamlet's activities, he urges them to lose no further time:

"*Delay it not* I'll have him hence tonight"

(italics added; IV.iii.5)

Later, while plotting with Laertes, he is again stricken with the fear that even though Laertes is apt and eager, he may conceivably lapse into delay; for there is always the possibility of a resolution slackening in the course of time. We 'should' do what we 'would' without letting time lapse.

.....for this would changes,
And hath abatements and delays as many
As there are tongues, are hands, are accidents;
And then this 'should' is like a spend-thrift's sigh
That hurts by easing......

(IV.vii.19 et seq)

This thought glances back ironically at the self-censuring soliloquy (IV.IV) where Hamlet questions:

I do not know
Why yet I live to say, This thing's to do;
Sith I have cause......

(43 et seq)

The stabbing sense of delay, common to both Hamlet and Claudius, connects with and accompanies the sense of being imperilled, which bed evils both. Claudius complains to Laertes of Hamlet having "pursued my life" (IV.vii.). In his conversation with Horatio, Hamlet is in a rage for Claudius having "thrown out his angle for my very proper life" (V.ii.6). When the prince is resolved not to "let this canker of our nature come/In further evil" (V.ii.69,70), Claudius is hatching his plot with Laertes to stop Hamlet once and for all from coming to further evil. If Claudius is to Hamlet a 'canker', Hamlet to Claudius is a 'foul disease'.

> ......Diseases desperate grown
> By desperate appliance are reliev'd,
> Or not at all
>
> (IV.iii.9 et seq)

Either, then, has problems in dealing promptly and effectively with his adversary. Claudius cannot take immediate steps for fear of alienating his queen and his subjects; Hamlet for "some craven scruple', or for 'thinking too precisely on the event' (IV. iv. 0,41), as he puts it once. Both thus suffer from a sense of impotent rage, though for different reasons.

If the sense of delay and the sense of jeopardy are common characteristics of both hero and villain, there is yet another way in which Shakespeare has given them ironically similar orientations. Indeed, it is interesting that both Claudius and Hamlet invoke a 'divinty' for their own purposes. The former feels assured of being protected by it (There's such divinity doth hedge a king/That treason can but peep to what it would,/Acts little of his will' (IV.v.120 et seq), while Hamlet attributes to it his miraculous escape : 'There's a divinity that shapes our ends'.

(V.ii.10)

The world of Hamlet is a world without issue. Even for Claudius who is neither 'remiss' nor 'generous' (the terms he uses for the prince) the much yearned for results remain ever out of sight. Each new move he initiates, each new scheme he devises is balked; and now, talking about the final gambit hit upon to eliminate Hamlet, he chuckles:

> I will work him
> To an exploit, now ripe in my device.
> Under the which he shall not choose but fall;
>
> (IV.vii.63 et seq.)

Significantly enough, Hamlet, who is often seen blundering (by the critics), goes about taking care of intruders and brokers with facility and decisiveness. He is clear in his mind about the situation making him act the way he does, as he sees it. It is a situation in which two mighty adversasies are pitted against each other, and he can have no scruples in sweeping away the baser elements that might be coming in the way. Looking at the corpse of Polonius, he remains remorseless and permits himself the following glib speech:

Thou wretched rash, *intruding* fool, farewell!
....
Thou fin'st to be too busy is some danger.

(italics added. III. iv. 3 et seq)

He is even more clear in his mind as to the justness of the fate he has sent his erst-while friends to:

Why, man, *they did make love to this employment;*
They are *not near my conscience;* their defeat
Does by their own insinuation grow.
'Tis dangerous when the *baser nature comes*
Between the pass and fell incensed point
Of mighty opposites.

(Italics added. V.ii.57 et seq)

Nevertheless, the action in question, the action to redeem his pledge proves hard to come by. To his consternation, he finds his rage getting expression more in words than in deed. He curses himself to reflect that 'like a whore' he should be condemned to "unpack my hearts with words" (II.ii.581).

It is significant in this context that Claudius too is alive to the all too natural human proclivity of seeking relief, however unconsciously, more in words than in actions. He asks Laertes:

What would you undertake
To show yourself indeed your father's son.
More than in words?

(Iv.vii.124 et seq)

It is worth-noting that Claudius's description of himself in his confessional soliloquy—

O limed soul, that, struggling to be free,
Art more engag'd!

(III.iii.68,69)

is true not merely of his inner self in its desperate need for God's forgiveness but also of his external situation where the more he perseveres, the greater is his frustration. In a way, his predicament is like that of Macbeth whose each single step in his chosen direction works for surer entanglement. All of Macbeth's actions in his struggle to escape from the fell net in which he is caught serve but to fasten him beyond all hope of release.

Both Claudius and Hamlet are tortured souls, in different ways though. Claudius's problem is the abortiveness of action, Hamlet's, the unavailability of it. For Claudius, even more than for Hamlet, it is a Kafka-world where every step taken is eventually a retrogression, where every fresh endeavour is to start from scratch, where all progression is a mirage, with the goal remaining tantalisingly out of reach. The Hamlet world is thus one where anxiety and dread dog man's footsteps; they are his perpetual companion.

This elaborate, though subtle, counterpointing of the tormented psychologies of hero and villain, this parallel enactment of their felt motives and perceived situations is the mechanism whereby Shakespeare directs attention to the dreadfulness of the dramatised world whose irremediable sterility can only be linked with fratricide and incest. It would appear to be a sovereign artistic commentary on the tangled situation in which the wrong-doer and the wronged are condemned to share an agony, which, arising from sacrilegious acts, has spread all over and spares none.

Before we take up the problem of delay as it relates to Hamlet (indeed, the problem is almost invariably seen exclusively in terms of Hamlet), it seems necessary that we take note of a phenomenon that seems close to Shakespeare's mind as it shapes the fictive world of *Hamlet.* That phenomenon pertains to time and the change that it works. It refers to the weakening and diminution of the elan behind an idea, a purpose in a world ruled by time. It fomulates the proposition that the lapse of time does, or is likely to, modify or even negate the action earlier decided on.

Thus Hamlet talks of himself as 'lapsd' in time and passion'. Claudius discourses on what might happen to a resolve spurred by love such as Laertes's if one left it to time:

> ....
> I know love is begun by time;
> And that I see, in passages of proof,
> Time *qualifies that spark and fire of it.*
> There lives within the very flame of love
> A *kind of wick or snuff that will abate it;*
> And nothing is at a like goodness still.
>
> (italics added, IV.vi. 111--16)

The player king dwells on the same thought:

> Purpose is but the slave to memory;
> Of violent birth, but poor validity:
> ....
> What to ourselves in passion we propose,

The passion ending, doth the purpose lose.

(III. ii. 183-90)

While this thought glances at the very basic malady that Hamlet harps on as the burden of his complaint (viz., the inconstancy of faith), it is of pointed relevance to the phenomenon of action becoming tardy, or not taking place at all. For action springs from passion or will, and once passion fades, the purpose wilts, and action either is not there, or if there at all, is tardy. The Hamlet world is pervasively coloured by this speculation.

In this respect, the world of *Othello* or *King Lear* is at a far remove from that of *Hamlet*. In neither of those two worlds is the possibility of a resolve lapsing into ineffectuality ever contemplated. To Iago's vicious dig that Othello's resolve may fade, the latter cries out:

Never, Iago. Like to the Pontic sea,
Whose icy current and compulsive course
Ne'er feels retiring ebb, but keeps due on
To the Propontic and the Hellespont;
Even so my bloody thoughts, with violent pace,
Shall ne'er look back, ne'er ebb to humble love
Till that a capable and wide revenge
Swallow them up.

(Italics added, Othello, III. iii 457 et seq)

Lear will not brook any interference with his will taking its inexorable course. He cant let anything "come betwixt our sentence and our power" and warns Kent to keep from meddling:

The bow is bent and drawn, make from the shaft.

(King Lear, I.i.142)

Compared to *Hamlet, Othello* and *Lear* represent a world where the springs of action are no longer choked, where the possibility of action is no longer in question. On the contrary, there is a new voilence, an irrepressible propensity to act. Indeed, it is a new menace.

In a still later play, *Macbeth,* where purpose is indeed conjoined with action, the earlier apprehension of time moderating the heat of a resolve is once more glimpsed. Hearing that Macduff has escaped to England, Macbeth chides himself for remissness:

Time, thou anticipat'st my dread exploits:
The flighty purpose never is o'ertook
Unless the deed go with it : from this moment
The very firstling of my heart shall be
The firstlings of my hand. And even now,

To crown my thoughs with acts, be it thought and done:

....

This deed I'll do before this purpose cool:

(*Macbeth* IV.i.144 et seq)

In *Antony and Cleopatra,* written around the same time, action has undergone a metamorphosis. It is now mortgaged to uxoriousness, a fatal infatuation. It is a travesty of itself.

III

We should now be trying to understand the nature and the cause of Hamlet's delay.

It has been noticed above how he makes short work of the wiles of the king's counsellor and agents engaged in robbing him of his secret. In fact, he gives them a short shrift with remarkable aplomb. Guarding his own secret, keeping his own being inviolable, hitting on a capital stratagem, he makes triumphantly certain his knowledge about his adversary's secret. Even though he is in a sense in enemy territory and even though he is subjected to mental torments, for his privacies are being intruded upon (one almost gets the impression that the prince is in a besieged garrison which is being sought to be surprised) he holds his ground with cool assurance and cunning and even, causes baffeled alarm in the mind of Claudius. This he succeeds in doing though sustained feats of calculated punning that takes on the dual aspect of inscrutabiltity and defiance, through the bold staging of the Gonzago play and though the ruthless disposal of the intruder who turns out to be Polonius. These acts together with the pugnacity of his bearing and the air of agression about his personality produce an unsettling effect upon the antagonist.

The plain fact is that Hamlet knows how to keep his counsel, how to act, how to tear into his enemy leaving him dismayed. The Coleridgean explanation that the delay is due to Hamlet's decidedly metaphysical turn of mind rendering him incapable of action obviously does not hold.

Why, then, is the delay in avenging the murder?

We shall in the course of our discussion take note of the theories of world weariness, of compunction and of irresolution. But before we come to that point it is necessary to recognise that Hamlet's acts until nearly the end of the play are of a different order from the act he is required to perform to get his revenge. His actions in the course of grappling with the enemy's moves are primarily aimed at self-survival and are preparatory to bracing himself up to redeem his pledge to the ghost. In other words, they are of a rather mundane, pedestrain character as compared with the other action expected of him—an action of extra-ordinary import and status. And that is so because the action he stands sworn to is commanded by a mysterious, invisible world and is meant to redeem and vindicate himself in his own esteem as also in the eyes of the supernatural order from where the apparition came. The extra-terrestrial origin of the command lends a new dimension to the task of revenge, investing it with an awesome aspect, and thus setting it distinctly, almost peremptorily, apart from whatever other actions in which Hamlet has found himself engaged in order to ensure his physical continuance in a rough and perilous world.

Now, the revelation of murder by the supernatural agency and the supernatural origin of the command to avenge distinguish *Hamlet* from the other revenge plays of the period. In those plays the agency of revelation is of this world and revenge is a task accepted by the hero of his own motion. In none of them is the task of revenge imposed by a Ghost, although such unearthly apparitions haunt the world.

Taking this aspect of the situation into account one may indeed suggest that the insurmountable difficulty for Hamlet is the dichotomy (and consequently the tension experienced) between the lack of inner assurance and the imperious command from an extraneous source. The obligation to rise against his uncle is more externally imposed that inwardly felt. This obviously is an entirely different situation from the one in which Hieronymo or Antonio or Vindice or Titus cries out for blood and displays steely resolve to act. Thus Prof. J.J.Lawlor sees in Hamlet "a man commanded to do what he has no assurance is right". And this situation, according to him, is one of 'pure tragedy".[1]

Now what is the evidence of the text? Even while Hamlet's task was not initially of his choosing, there is not a scrap of evidence after the Gonzago-play to support the view that Hamlet still doubts the bonafides of the Ghost or that his conscience resists what he is oath-bound to accomplish. On the otherhand, he had his suspicions about his uncle even before the spectral disclosure which came only to confirm them. Moreover, he continually castigates himself for not doing what he should have done, not only because he has been commanded to do so but more because he feels inwardly impelled to do it as the only means of discharging a son's obligation to the beloved father so treacherously murdered. What, for example, does Hamlet mean by the question:

> He that hath kill'd my king and whor'd my mother;
> Popp'd in between th' election and my hopes;
> Thrown out his angle for my proper life,

And with such coz'nage,......
And is't not to be damn'd
....
To let this canker of our nature come
In further evil?

(V.ii.64 et seq)

On this showing, it is true to say that there is no friction, no discordance at all between the external command and his inner voice and that his entire soul gives assent to the ghost's exhortation. The call from without becomes a call from within.Thus, the suggestion that Hamlet is without an inner assurance can only be seen to betray a presumption unauthenticated by the text.

The cause of Hamlet's delay, then, must be sought elsewhere. Pertinent to any discussion on this aspect is what his uncle and his mother have done, robbing him of his faith in man and woman ('man delights me not; no, nor woman neither' II. ii. 308), in fact, of the very ground of his existence. A man who has been struck spiritually vacuous has hardly any urge to live, far less to act. It is worth noting that a deep cynicism has overtaken Hamlet even before the stunning revelation of the murder. The ways of the world, such as he has been a witness to, have left him high and dry in a state of spiritual wilderness. He longs for a winding up of the business of life.

O, that this too too solid flesh would melt,

(.ii. 129)

In the meantime the unearthly visitor has come and gone, bringing confirmation to his 'prophetic' soul and leaving his mind in a whirl. And once again we hear Hamlet bewail his lot

The time is out of joint O cursed spite,
That ever I was born to set it right!

(I.v.189,190)

We have already noticed the unusual nature of the intimation of the crime and of the command to act. This unusual feature of the play has to be seen as accounting for Hamlet's whirling agitation, sometimes verging on frenzy, for what be calls the 'excitements of my reason and my blood'. Coming from a supernatural region, the command to act causes an enormous friction between a mode of life, already affected by the incipience of cynicism and premonition and the newly released compulsion to renounce his old self and to forge a sensibility geared singly to the only meaningful task ahead of him.

The resulting psychic inflammation, evidences of which can easily be culled from his reactions and speeches, does not, however, impede for long a meaningful conduct of affairs. He has already decided to 'put an antic disposition on' in order to achieve his end. Even the great death-centred soliloquy—'To be, or not to be' contemplates action as a serious proposition. ("Or to take arms against a sea of troubles,/And by opposing end them"). Hamlet's world-weariness never inhibits action—his modes of action. He is already up and about in his assumed role of a lunatic jester. The arrival of the players boosts up his soul and he is now revived, if only for the purpose of effecting his mission.

One of the principal ironies in the play is when Claudius welcomes the news that the players "have already order/This-night to play before him" and that Hamlet entreats "your Majesties/To hear and see the matter". "With all my heart; and it doth much content me/To hear him so inclin'-d"(III.i,20 et seq)—responds Claudius. The motive and import of Hamlet's action completely elude him. But how does the prince himself perceive the situation and the nature of his task?

It may be of use at this stage to compare Hamlet with the heroes of other revenge plays of the same period. The avenging heroes are, as a rule, seized with a kind of unholy glee in going about their self-appointed task. Hamlet is not.

In *The Spanish Tragedy*, Hieronymo who has lived by conscience and the law is not quite different from his enemy in moral texture towards the end. In *Antonio's Revenge* Antonio stabs the murderer's son displaying all the elements of an appalling melodrama :

> Me thinks I pace upon front of Jove,
>
> (III.iii)

In *The Revenger's Tragedy*, Vindice is forced to assume the disguise of a pander to Lussurioso. His task of revenge involves the need to be treacherous to his mother and sister. In Shakespeare's own *Titus Andronicus* Titus has to serve Tamora with the flesh of her own sons. They are all sucked into the whirlpool of evil. Vindice's summing up: "For to be honest is not to be i' the world" could serve as the motto for the rest of the avengers. They are seen to embrace the very things they arraign. They get tainted with the vice around and they sink to the lowest depths of immorality to achieve their ends.

From such avengers Hamlet stands apart and he does so by virtue of a dour moral vision that would be incomprehensible to them. Where Vindice tempts his sister Castiza:

How blessed are you! You have happiness alone;
Others must fall to thousands, you to one,
Sufficient in himself to make your forehead
Dazzle the world with jewels, and petitionary people
Start at your presence.....
hurry, hurry, hurry—

(*The Revenger's Tragedy*, II.i.)

Hamlet is exhorting Ophelia to get to a nunnery, a place where she would be beyond the reach of calumny and stain and he is counselling abstinence to his mother who is deep in vice.

The moral texture thus exhibited is in keeping with the fact that when he happens to kill Polonius and later when he sends Rosencrantz and Guildenstern to their death, he does not draw blood in full sight of his victims. In the case of Polonius he blindly makes a thrust through the arras—a highly impulsive action performed without deliberation. In the other case, there is deliberation, but he is provoked to the deed by the sudden revelation of treachery. Indeed, in both cases there is immediate provocation. He would seem to need such immediate provocation to rise against Claudius. One feels that Brutus's self-portraiture aptly fits Hamlet. The picture is of one

Who, much enforced, shows a hasty spark,
And straight is cold again

(*Julius Caesar* IV.iii)

Murderous action, then, is something he would naturally avoid unless it is forced upon him by the resistless compulsion of the moment. This, in a way, brings us to the compunction theory according to which the prince is delayed by his fine scruple in taking the step he is being expected to take. Shakespeare's Hamlet, a Renaissance young intellectual, is far removed from the young hero of Saxo Grammaticus dispensing wild justice uninhibited by compunction. Peter Alexander writes:

> ......the imperative duty of seeing the wild justice done that only a cowardly and disloyal son could shirk and the compunction that a humaner tradition imposes, are....at war in Hamlet's soul; these are the elements that engage in the kind of fighting that will not let Hamlet rest".[2]

While the above statement puts the matter in perspective, it yet falls short of getting at the matter adequately. In this connection, we may profitably recall the following words of Charles Williams:

> Action, after all, is a very difficult thing. The normal acts of our lives are either habitual or compulsory. Either we act as we are used to act or circumstances compel us to some unaccustomed act. The extreme of our choice is to do or to refrain, bu the deed is usually a mere variation on our ordinary deeds.....But the finality of killing, the strangeness of the act of killing, imposes on us the need for a deeper impulse, an impulse which normally demands intensely vivid circumstances before it can be set in motion, and an intense profit to ourselves from the deed. Of the forgery of the death warrant for Rosencrantz and Guildenstern we might all be capable. But the necessity laid on Hamlet is even heavier it is to find out a way to act where his own profit is not concerned—it is literally to act disinterestedly, from free will.[3].

Williams would seem to define the situation with absolute perspicacity. The action demanded of Hamlet is neither a habitual or customary act, nor such as is triggered by the immediate compulsion of the moment, nor again such as one performs from a sense of profit. The action demanded is of an entirely differnt character. Such an action can only take place in a state of complete disinterestedness and with the full and unqualified approval of the entire being. It demands a unique sort of 'readiness' such as Hamlet talks of on the eve of the fencing match with Laertes. And such readiness is not easy to come by.

Unlike the other acts, the act of revenge concerns the centrality of Hamlet's being. The contemplation of it drives him irresistibly to his insistent awareness and apprehension of himself, of what constitutes his essence—that irreducible sum of elements lending dignity and worth and grace to his status as man and providing the sole justification for not calling himself 'a beast, no more'. It is important to note that Hamlet has given us the invaluable benefit of his focus on man at more than one place:

> What a piece of work is man ! How noble in reason ! how infinite in faculties!......In action, how like an angel! in apprehension how like a god! the beauty of the world!
>
> (II.ii. 300 et seq)
>
> Sure he that made us with such large discourse,
> Looking before and after, gave us not
> That Capability and god-like reason
> To fust in us unus'd.
>
> (IV. iv. 36 et seq)

In is true that the ebullience of this vision has suffered an eclipse. Gaping and ugly fissures have appeared in that vision to cause dismay and cynicism. In fact, the play is, in large measure, about the travesty and fall of an ideal which now appears to have been built on too confident a premise. Nevertheless, the prince who envisions man in such glowing terms has to be true to his cherished vision in the face of all distortions that mock it. His innate sense of human worth and dignity, he alone can and will exemplify and uphold in his conduct, especially in that single awesome task that has been assigned to him. The assignment of the task has elicited an eager, breathless response; it has the approval of the whole movement of his soul by oath bent on to revenge.

Thus, to define his role as an avenger we have to keep in mind Hamlet's harping on those high attributes which set man apart from a brute. How god-like he can be in apprehension, in understanding ! How angelic in action ! And Hamlet is a young man who has seen man in that aspect, clothed with that glory, and has thrilled to see that high vision which *ipso facto* is excluded from the world in which animal actions hold unrestricted sway. Hamlet can be trusted to have given his entire allegiance to his lofty notion of man. Now when he addresses himself to the supreme task before him, a task intended to test him as a man, can he conceivably afford to ignore the demands of 'such large discourse', that 'god-like reason' obligating him to "look before and after' and to make the most judicious exercise of the freedom of choice implicit in and emanating from the faculty of reason ? In this the most momentous task, how well and honourably does he acquit himself ? He must needs be worthy of the image of man he himself has held up before us and that is how he can justify or vindicate it.

He is in possession of an ideal that stands sullied by the court. And his being in possession of it explains why he cannot sink low and wallow in the mire in avenging his father, why he cannot do by hook or by crook what he has undertake to do; why, in other words, he cannot be a conventional aveger who soon ceases to be morally superior to his victim.

Hamlet, then, must discrimnate between what is right action and what is not. Any action at any time and at any place will not meet the ends of justice as he sees it. An act of revenge heedless of time and place, i.e. regardless of the circumstantial factors, would be just 'hire and salary, not revenge.' Such an action would be 'scanned'. He will let go the opportunity (provided by the defenceless Claudius at prayer) which is no opportunity at all except to a blood thirsty avenger blind to reasons and unaware of the true implication of choice.

So, then, Hamlet will choose the moment to strike. And on his own testimony:

...... I have cause, and will, and strength and means
To do't.

(IV, Iv. 44,45).

On his own testimony, too, there is delay. Time flies past and the deed remains undone. He chides, flagellates himself. He is flagellating his mother in the closet scene when the Ghost reappears. And how does he react?,

Do you not come your tardy son to chide,
That laps'd i time ad passion, lets go by
The important acting of the dread command?

(III. ib. 106 et seq)

For however brief a while, the focus of reproach shifts from his mother to himself; he has replaced his mother with himself as the recipient of biting censure:

Then he sees Fortinbras leading an expedition to capture a tiny piece of land

Exposing what is mortal and unsure
To all that fortune, death, and danger dare,
Even for an egg-shell.

(IV vi 51 et Seq)

and he is stung with bitter self-reproach:

.... How stand I, then,
That have a father kill'd a mother 'Staind
Excitements of my reason and my blood,
And let all sleep.......? ....

(IV.iv. 56 et seq)

He has earlier in the same soliloquy had a dig at himself:

... What is a man,
If his chief good and market of his time
Be but to sleep and feed?

(Iv. iv. 34 et seq)

And later after his "sudden and most strange return" from the voyage which was to have seen the end of him, Hamlet, while giving a recital of his dreadful experience to Horatio, exclaims;

.... is't not perfect conscience
To quit him (Claudius) with this arm?

(V.ii. 67, 78)

The point in citing these damningly confessional statements is that Hamlet is seen to be beset with a gnawing perplexity (being unable to fathom why there cotinues to be a gap between intent and action), that there is a persisting lack of proper equation between him and the reality, the latter withholding what the former demands. He has the agony without the light which alone could show its place in a state of poised contemplation. Yet an outsider to the heart of the universe, he is, in Keatsean phraseology, in the "Chamber of Maiden thought" on all sides of which "many doors are set open-but all dark-all leading to dark passages-we see not the ballance (sic) of good and evil. We are in a Mist."[4]

Shakespeare creates the tension between expectations roused and their realisation denied, or rather, delayed. This tension goes deeper than and beyond what may perhaps be called a characteristic feature of a revenge play in which the avenger coventionally takes rather long to complete his task. This tension is meant to illuminate what is at the heart of the play-the anguished dilemma of the protagonist to whose exclusive perception of his task the world remains unresponsive. Hamlet's percipience renders his job especially difficult in the sense that he wants his mission carried out in a manner which is resisted, even opposed by the contrary character of the existential situation (One might as well put this dualism or dichotomy in terms of the dense, recalcitrant matter resiting the spirit's plastic stress). Not only in the external world but even at the plane of epistemology there is a war, if unstated, between Hamlet and his world. He has to subordinate it to a higher knowledge which is yet to dawn.

Hamlet obviously conceives of his projected revenge as a ritual act (the prompting having emanated from the other world) to be performed with a sense of adequacy and fulfilment. He must not only perform the act, but perform it at an appropriately chosen moment; that is, the performance of it would leave him unstatisfied, even unfulfilled, if it did not conform to the norm lodged in and dictated by his imagination. This is precisely where he is unlike the general run of avengers who indeed have to look fairly long for the opportuity to strike which is provided, as in Hamlet, by the victim himself, but who never known the dilemma if only because they have never known that moral vision. For them revenge is little better than killing, or murder, the nature of the killing being of no relevance or consequence whatever. For Hamlet, the nature of the killing is of supreme importance. He is all for 'revenge' as he understands it, not for 'hire and salary' which most acts of revenge are, to his way of looking at the problem.

Neither Laertes nor Fortinbras, both of whom are spurred by the motive of revenge in their own ways, suffers from anything like the dilemma that afflicts Hamlet. In IV. vii. where Claudius and Laertes are plotting against Hamlet's life, the terms in which the King sets forth his notion of revenge serve to throw into sharp relief Hamlet's idea of revenge. 'No. place, indeed', affirms the king, 'should murder sanctuarise;/Revenge should have no bounds.'

(IV. vii. 127, 128)

In his eyes revenge and murder are synonymous and one could carry out murder by way of taking revenge just any where and at any time without turning a hair. There need be no compunction felt about the time and place of killing. The question of discrimination just does not enter. As for Laertes, as he has already put it, he would not scruple "to cut his (Hamlet's) throat" i'th' church".

(IV. vii,. 126)

Thus for Hamlet it is not blind vengeance. His act of revenge should be an act of free choice exercised in the light of reason. Such an act alone would be worthy of him, the compulsive expounder of reason. But such an act is not easy to perform. Which explains the fretful waiting, and it is entirely misleading to suggest that the play is about a young man who has never been able to make up his mind. Hamlet has never wavered in his resolution especially since he 'caught the conscience' of the king, thanks to the 'Mouse-trap'. His mind is long made up about the task which he has accepted with a sense of religiosity and from which he has not even once recoiled in thought.

But while the inviolable resolution is already there, a commesurate free act in execution of that resolution cannot come when the mind remains in a state of agitation, or as long as it remains enmeshed in the toils of cogitation, i. e., in the processes of discursive reasoning, linking up perceptions and weighing and balancing. Discursive reason, while being the mainstay of the human mind in the process of evaluating experience, of judging a situation and reaching conclusions in the practical affairs of life, ceases to be of help at the higher plane where the factors governing action are no loger pragmatic or utilitarian and where the concerns are absolute and not relative with such considerations as of loss and gain having been superseded by the more fundamental demands of the inner life.

Hamlet's excited reflections on the agony of the human situation, his comparing himself, to his own disadvantage, with the player simulating Hecuba's passion and with Fortinbras ready to stake everything for the sake of an 'egg-shell' are only the workings of discursive reason or what Keats calls 'consequtive reasoning' which can never enable him to achieve a total inside view of his situation because it is bat-eyed, dim of vision. Such congitations can only serve to fasten him further in the externality of things. He has to look inward and find his place in the scheme of things which is his own and no one else's. Every man's place unnder the sun, every man's destiny, is his own and no one else's.

This realisation is the gift of a higher faculty. Intuitive or higher reason yields a synoptic vision which alone can enable Hamlet to recognise his place with clarity, a place not to be mistaken either for that of the player referred to above or of Fortinbras. That vision will help him muster a new orientation where he is no longer a fevered, fragmented and dismembered self. It will help him achieve an integration within himself and a harmony with the universe. It alone can bring him the equanimity, that spirit of self-possession which will be the mother of the act he has been looking for in vain.

Talking of the glory that is man, Hamlet had exclaimed: "in action, how like an angel!' Now angels are possessed not of discursive but intuitive reason which gives them an immediate vision of things as a whole resulting in immediate and effortless action. Distinguishing the immediate character of intuitive, angelic apprehension from the mediated nature of human knowledge, C.S. Lewis observes:

A congnitive life in which all truth can be simply seen would be the life of an *intelligentia*, and angel. A life of an unmitigated, *ratio* where nothing was simply 'seen' and all had to be proved, would presumably be impossible; for nothing can be proved if nothing is self-evident. Man's mental life is spent in laboriously connecting those frequent, but momentary flashes of intelligentia which constitute *intellectus*.[5]

Hamlet has to wait for that angelic mode of apprehension, which need only operate in a flash to pave the way for the action he wants. In such an event, he will be driven by an illumination which will free him from his inner wrestle and make him 'see into the life of things'. It will put him in possession of the truth of what Oceanus expounds in *Hyperion*:

To bear all naked truths
To envisage circumstance, all calm,
That is the top of sovereignty.

Oceanus expounds the truth of self-possession,of distinterestedness. Of this distinterestedness Krishna spoke to Arjuna in the Bhagvad Gita. And Arjuna could bring himself to act only when he achieved a kind of mental elevation, of self-possession rising above the accidents and attachment of life. Williams, in the passage quoted earlier, has this disinterestedness to stress. When such disinterestedness springs in the mind, the clog to action goes and there is complete release and surrender. This, indeed, is the state of true freedom in which action comes almost unbidden and with spontaneity. As D.H. Lawrence writes so movingly, though in a different context:

Men are free when they are obeying some deep, inward voice of religious belief. Obeying from within. Men are free when they belong to a living, organic, believing community, active in fulfilling some unfulfilled, perhaps unrealised purpose..... Men are free when they are most unconscious of freedom.... Men are only free when they are doing what the deepest self likes. And there is getting down to the deepest self. It takes some diving. Because the deepest self is way down, and the conscious self is an obstinate monkey.[6]

Hamlet gains this deeper freedom and the spontaneous impulse for action following his return from the providentially interrupted voyage. The sea is recurrently the symbol of renewal and rebirth in Shakespeare. One has only to look at such plays as *Twelfth Night, Pericles, The Winter's Tale* and *The Tempest*. Separation and loss are transfigured into union and rejuvenation. The prince who had been sent away to die and who should not have been heard of any more comes with a new accent of life and faith. He speaks a new idiom, the idiom of intuitive understanding, of integration. One who had been alienated comes to be aligned to a "living, organic, believing community" of souls. He sees, as he never did before, a purpose running through creation, a providence. He talks of a divinity shaping our end, so that what might appear to be a 'rash', 'indiscreet' action is basically prompted by a benign, pervasive intelligence shaping things to a pre-determined end. He talks of 'heaven' being 'ordinant' in his discovering the king's treachery and in sending the two spies to the fate that had been designed for him. And, finally, when he avers: "The readiness is all' (V. ii. 215) we hear the accent of a soul that has moved past all inner wrestle and achieved self-possession and equanimity. We can almost hear the ring of finality about the assertion- 'The readiness is all'. The soul is postured in a state of readiness whether to act or to die, according as the call comes from within.

The climactic voyage that has bred this attitude marks a sea-change in the character of time. Time that was barren and unyielding for the alienated soul recovers meaning with the alien becoming an integral part of the scheme of things. Arguing on entirely different lines, Frederick Turner reaches a similar conclusion on the new beneficence of time:

> Hamlet has regained his faith; in particular his faith in Providence as the effect on time of a beneficent timeless world. And this faith in Providence is justified: time, which at first had seemed disrupted by the appearance of the Ghost, and later the stumbling-block and

> insurmountable limitation of his revenge, now sweeps Hamlet into his victory with enormous momentum.[7]

The revelation of treachery, as the fencing match is on, is the opportunity provided by the newly fruitful time for Hamlet to redeem himself. And Hamlet is equal to it, the act being witness to the coinciding of intellectual clarity, moral certainty and spiritual cohesion.

The ancient mariner must integrate himself into the living universe before his 'becalmed' ship can move again. Prometheus must resurrect love in his heart before he can see his adversary fall. Hamlet has to re-orient himself before he can achieve the last, 'mystic' act of his life. And just as Samson brushes aside the choric expostulation and answers the Philistine summons and Becket dismisses the priestly advice not to face the assassins, even so Hamlet rejects Horatio's prudential counsel and goes out to meet his destiny. 'Readiness' is the word for them all. They have put all calculation behind.

We must, however, end with a note of caution. Unlike in the case of a Samson or a Becket, the upsurge and effect of faith are rather transitory in the case of Hamlet. While they have left all worldly considerations clean behind themselves, Hamlet, immediately after he has accomplished his revenge, is a disconsolate soul: it occurs to him that his life comes to a premature end and that his reputation is at stake.

> Had I but time, as this fell sergeant Death
> Is strict in his arrest, O, I could tell you-
> But let it be. Horatio, I am dead:
> ...... report me and my cause aright
> To the unsatisfied.
>
> (V.ii. 328 et seq)

The rousing faith which had swept him on to action takes leave of him. Unlike the protagonists of religious plays, Hamlet dies as a man of the world, a Renaissance figure, with a lingering attachment to the world and with obvious note of regret for not being able to clear his name of likely aspersions. The sovereign moment which saw the coincidence of a decisive movement of his soul and the malleability of the external situation, is now a thing of the past, and the old discordance takes its place. And this is so because of the reassertion of the secular spirit with its focus on society and an accomplished individual's place in it with his sense of honour and reputation. The Renaissance prince's sense of wounded reputation now takes precedence over all else. When Hamlet stops Horatio from drinking whatever remains of the poison, he has left the company of heroes such as we have compared him with. He has reassumed his secular self. And for a secular hero the world remains important but recalcitrant in its character. To Samson and Beckett, considerations that make for Hamlet's complaint would make no meaning at all. They leave the world behind as of no consequence now. Hamlet dies,not detached, but with his eyes lowered and therefore with a muted protest against the world that denies him full satisfaction in accomplishing his revenge. And here the play belongs to the general pattern and ethics of Shakespeare's tragedies.

REFERENCES

1. "The Tragic Conflict in Hamlet' *Review of English Studies*, N.S. I. (1950), pp. 97-113.
2. *Shakespeare*, The English Language Book Society & O.U.P., 1965. p. 222.
3. *Shakespeare Criticism* (1919-35), The World's Classies, ed. Ann. Ridler, pp. 205-6.
4. Letter to J.M. Reynolds, May 3, 1818. See*The Letters of John Keats*,ed. H.E. Rollins, 2 vols., Camb. Mass. 1958.
5. *The Discarded Image*, An Introduction to Medieval and Renaissance Literature, C.U.P. 1964, p. 157.
6. "The Spirit of Place', *'Studies in Classic American literature*, Penguin Books, 1971, pp. 12-13.
7. *Shakespeare and the Nature of Time*, O.U.P., 1971 p. 98.

OPHELIA AND THE CRITICS

Ophelia is the odd person out among Shakespeare's women. The basic fact about her is her lack of self-assertion, her inability or disinclination to act. Therefore, the basic critical problem about her is: Why is this lack or attrition of will, what could possibly be its cause? In other words, the ciritical enquiry should aim at identifying that something in the existential situation or in its ambience which might seem satisfactorily to explain this singular phenomenon of her not acting upon the promptings of her heart. For the promptings are obvious and what is equally obvious is that she chooses to treat them rather casually, if not stifle them altogether, giving rise to a neurosis- the result of repressed sexuality-to which some of her mad songs bear witness.

It is an indisputable fact in Shakespeare that in matters amorous a woman listens more to the inner voice-an imperious one-than to any counselling from without. We would not have stressed this point if Ophelia had not known love. She knows it.

> And I, of ladies most deject and wretched,
> That suck'd the honey of his music vows,
> ....
> O, woe is me,
> T' have seen what I have seen, see what I see;
> (III.i. 155 et. seq.)

Yet, critics never tire of harping on Ophelia's innocence. Dr. Johnson refers to her as "the young, the beautiful, the harmless, and the pious". Lamb speaks of the "loving intercourse which is broken off by Hamlet through "affected discourtesies". Bradley dwells on her "childlike innocence". Kitto records her "innocent obedience". And so run the encomia.

The question that should necessarily arise is: 'well, innocent of what'? Ophelia is certainly not innocent of love, even though she may be innocent of the evils of the world. And to be fair, none of the critics cited above would dispute that she has experienced the emotion of love in some measure or other. And if she is not innocent of love, then this talk of innocence is simply beside the point or misdirected. If she is innocent in the sense that there is a virginal purity about her, all other Shakespearean heroines of about her age have it too and, therefore, they are no less innocent than Ophelia. None of them is a wanton. And one does not need a wanton to demonstrate the force and passion of love. She is innocent as any other woman in Shakespeare is innocent, and she is not innocent of love as Juliet or Julia or Desdemona or Miranda or Perdita is not. Where Ophelia is different from other women in a similar situation is that while the latter act, she does not.

On the estrangement of Hamlet and Ophelia, Lamb maintains that Hamlet employed a "profound artifice of love" which consisted in "alienating Ophelia by affected discourtesies in order to break off that loving intercourse which can no longer find a place amidst business so serious as that which he has to do".[1]

Dr. Johnson views the character and death of Ophelia as follows:

> "........ the gratification which would arise from the destruction of an usurper and a murderer, is abated by the untimely death of Ophelia, the young, the beautiful, the harmless, and the pious".[2]

The present essay will take into account and examine the validity of such opinions, among others, with the object of exploring Shakespeare's presentation of the complex relationship between Hamlet and Ophelia, of Ophelia's tragedy and how integral it is to the scheme of the play.

There is an unconscious irony in Gertrude's speech to Ophelia in Act III Sc. I, coming as it does when the latter is going to be used as a 'decoy' in the nunnery-scene:

> And for your part, Ophelia, I do wish
> That your good beauties be the happy cause
> Of Hamlet's wildness: so shall I hope your virtues
> Will bring him to his wonted way again,
> To both your honours.
>
> (38 et. seq.)

Already for Hamlet, 'beauties' in a woman are a key to her being dishonest; Ophelia's 'virtues' are already ashes in his mouth and his 'wildness' is going to break into a tempest of sarcastic fury in the encounter with her to follow.

Ophelia's tragedy and Hamlet's are mainfestly inter-related, yet it needs stressing that they offer one of the subtlest studies in contrast that the play offers. She is fatally unaware of the nature of the world she is in a world which impinges on her subtly with a crippling effect and of the inner world of Hamlet which is compulsively transferred to and read in the world without. Hamlet is aware of evil, she is not. He is a pronounced individualist, a non-conformist; she conforms facilely. He displays a remarkable passion of thought and inclination. Whatever subterranean passion Ophelia may have experienced for Hamlet is never channelled into a decided course of action. She has never known that rebellion, that adhesive clinging to and pursuit of an uncharted path in imperious response to the urgings of the soul, which Shakespeare's heroines have made familiar to us almost as a rule of conduct. She is the only heroine who plays her father's game only to succeed in making immeasurably worse what was already for her a bad enough situation. She dies frustrated, unfulfilled, uncomprehending and ignorant. Hamlet's tragedy marks a transition from ignorance to knowledge punctuated with a tempestuous, if ineffectual, expenditure of energy. Lady Macbeth turns into a somnambulist and dies only after she has given a decisive exhibition of her character. Ophelia goes mad and dies following a life of fatuous dependence and of a pathetic inability to face herself.

In Act II Sc. I Ophelia reports to her father an incident in which Hamlet seems to have behaved pretty abnormally bursting into her chamber:

> As if he had been loosed out of hell
> To speak of horrors
>
> (83-84)

Ophelia's description, vivid and meticulous, leaves us in no doubt that Hamlet's conduct did show a complete loss of self-control, that it was no play-acting but the expression of an ungovernable storm in his mind. As Ophelia's image suggests, Hamlet must have had, as it were, an experience of being in hell accounting for the absolute loss of his bearings and the conduct almost of one demented. What is that experience and how does one explain it[7]?

In an earlier scene (Act I Sc. III) Ophelia tells her father :

> He hath, my lord, of late made many tenders
> Of his affection to me.
>
> (99-100)

> My lord, he hath importun'd me with love
> In honourable fashion
>
> (110-111)

> And hath given countenance to his speech, my lord,
> With almost all the holy vows of heaven.
>
> (113-114)

The emphasis on the 'honourable' character of it is significant. There is, be it noted, nothing slimy or underhand about it. It is such love as receives the seal of approval from man and God. So that it does not call for hedging or concealment. But Polonius would have none of it. With vulgar cynicism he exclaims:

> Affection: pooh; you speak like a green girl (101)
> Ay. springes to catch woodcocks. (115)

Here is a man who does not believe in anything fresh and sacred, anything that has issued unalloyed from the deep warmth of the heart. He understands 'policy', 'practice'. 'Do not believe his vows', he warns, 'for they are brokers'. And finally he delivers the injunctions:

> I would not, in plain terms, from this time
> forth have you so slander any moment leisure
> As to give words or talk with the Lord Hamlet,
> Look to't, I charge you.
>
> (132 et. seq.)

Ophelia vows obedience, though one is right to suspect that she is shocked and her heart shrinks. In strict obedience, she goes about discouraging Hamlet and his advances. In Act 11 Sc. I she informs her father:

> .... as you did command,
> I did repel his letters, and denied
> His access to me.
>
> 11.i (108 et seq.)

Hamlet's mind is already in a whirl on account of Gertrude's conduct. His mother's hasty and incestuous marriage has given too rude a jolt for him to believe any longer in a woman's constancy, in her fidelity. And now comes another experience to fill to the brim his cup of cynicism. Ophelia round whom he has been weaving his fond dream of the future is no longer her former-self. She has begun to treat him as an unwelcome stranger, forgetting how warmly she had reciprocated his love in the past. His world now goes to pieces. He sees horrors round him. He is, as it were, in hell, undergoing all the torments of it. It is a maddeningly frightening vision comparable to Blake's vision of London.

Thus what Lamb calls 'that loving intercourse' has been brought to an end, but this has been done not, as he maintains, by Hamlet by 'a profound' artifice of love' (referring to his seeming antics in the nunnery scene), but by Ophelia herself through her self-defeating compliance with her father's prohibitory ruling. She has already alienated him and his love is dead. When he resorts to the so-called 'affected discourtesies', their 'loving intercourse' is already a thing of the past.

A profound emotional and moral crisis shakes and nearly over-turns his physical frame. Ophelia's description reflects this shattered Hamlet. In an uncontrollable mood of going over the wreck of his love and hopes ('the pangs of despised love') he comes running to Ophelia, in an unconsciously macabre revelation of his unhinged mind through the sartorial disorder, to look at her, to see what she really looks like, to make certain whether it is the same girl that had returned and reciprocated his love only yesterday. He is completedly woe-begone (Ophelia used the epithet 'piteous' twice). He stares with unbelief and despair at the final wreckage of his love, his hope, his life.

He rais'd a sigh so piteous and profound
As it did seem to shatter all his bulk
And end his being.

II.i (94 et seq.)

To be sure, the abnormal, if mournful, particulars of conduct that Ophelia refers to have nothing to do with Hamlet's resolution to 'put an antic disposition on'. These are the authentic expressions of the broken spirit within him, of his stricken inner self, They do not 'seem'. They denote him truly; they are'not actions that a man might play'. These have nothing to do with his assumed role in the play. The anguished vision from which sprang the generalised cry, 'frailty, they name is woman' has now acquired a fresh dimension of horror, past mitigation and repair. Polonius is indeed mistaken in concluding that he has got at the heart of Hamlet's mystery. "I have", he tells the king, "found the very cause of Hamlet's lunacy".

Let us now approach Hamlet's encounter with Ophelia in Act III Sc. I. we should approach the scene with the knowledge that his disillusion is complete and his cynicism has gained a new astringency. In this encounter Hamlet starts on a note of sarcasm He has a fresh remembrance of being treated atrociously by Ophelia, who, as she herself reported to her father, had "repelled his letters, and denied his access". The paroxysm of grief which he had displayed in his last meeting with her is over. He has pulled himself together, at least to all intents and purposes.

There is certainly a touch of irony in his address:

The fair Ophelia. -Nymph, in thy orisons
Be all my sins rememb'red.

(89)

Experience has driven home to him the certainty that a fair exterior hides corruption. The example of his mother's conduct and the more recent example of Ophelia's back-sliding, be it at her father's bidding, have carried conviction to him beyond a doubt. He is being ironical in his further references to her as a 'nymph' and to his own sins whatever they are. Hamlet undoubtedly is playing,with however heavy a heart, his assumed role-that of a witty jester.

In Hamlet's- 'I humbly thank you; well, well, well', a cryptic note of formality has already crept in and with it a note of disrelish, of indifference (........... well, well, well)

When Ophelia, with a touch of wounded vanity, announces her intention to return all his gifts, Hamlet promptly denies having given her any, that is, he disowns the past relationship in answer to her rejection of his love. He registers Ophelia's perversity, her brazen cussedness. He notes how wantonly she side-tracks her own responsibility for the collapse of their relationship. He sees her guilty of unseemly cunning, of patent dishonesty in putting the blame on him, while wearing the mask of one sinned against. Kitto, who, as we noted at the outset,finds Ophelia 'innocently obedient', goes on to uphold her conduct in relation to Hamlet. There is nothing wrong, according to him, in her returning the gifts on the instructions of her father. In fact, her doing so is a point in her favour. She remains untainted.

"Polonius, true to his character, has 'loosed her to him', but she is unaware of this and is untainted by his coarseness. Instructed to be in the lobby by a certain hour to see Hamlet, she gives back the memorials of a love that has been killed. By whom? Not by her fault, unless it is a fault in a daughter to be obedient to a wise father".[3]

further:

"It may not be logical in Ophelia.... to reproach Hamlet with being unkind, but surely it is not in the least unnatural if she, being herself so innocent, should think reproachfully of him, that he should not have persisted in spite of the obstacle".[4]

To Kitto, Ophelia is "desperately sincere" and she acts in "complete sincerity and innocence".

Our answer to this criticism would be that daughters in love do not remain obedient to their 'wise' fathers, for it is Shakespeare himself who has erected this into a rule. To been an exception to it would suggest something seriously wrong in such a daughter, some grave deficiency.

After having realised and reported to her father that her lover is utterly distraught, Ophelia should have known better than to allow herself to do anything that might conceivably exacerbate his feelings further. It suggests a complete lack of intelligence, if not a most lamentable servility to her father or sheer perversity to go the way she does. In her situation she should have taken the initiative by breaking loose from her father to stand beside her lover, instead of making a virtue of obedience and putting obstacles in his way to see if he can overcome them.

Finally, a truly innocent girl would simply not take to play-acting and see her lover move out of her orbit just to please a 'wise'father. Being in love, no matter how innocent one is of the evil around, admits of no such innocence. Play-acting on one's own makes sense but not when it is done at the instance of a 'wise' father.

This procedure, to Hamlet's searching mind, is less than fair. Hence the ironic grin:

> Ha, ha: are you honest?
> ....
> Are you fair?

To a puzzled and uncomprehending Ophelia, Hamlet's answer that honesty, supposing she is possessed of it, should keep her beauty at an arm's length, causes further confusion. The bitterly witty cynicism of it is more than Ophelia can comprehend or admit. Hamlet's answer to her next query even surpasses the ferocity of his earlier observation; the power of beauty, as has been experientially known by him, will sooner infect and transform honesty than the force of honesty can draw beauty towards itself. Hamlet's 'Ay, truly' is indeed said with withering scorn. The relationship between beauty and honesty as Hamlet expounds it was sometime a paradox, 'but now the time gives it proof'.

(II.i 114)

The implied suggestion cannot but be too shocking for Ophelia to accept. Hamlet did love Ophelia when beauty held a wholesome traffic with honesty, when they were twins. They are no longer so. With the basis for love gone, his love has withered too. There is now a sudden flash of an all consuming revelation in which the human world appears as a wasteland in which nothing wholesome can ever flourish or take root. Hamlet's mind touches the very depths of despair. His thoughts suggest the height of cynicism. With an air of deadly finality he pronounces the whole human stock rotten beyond repair and rejuvenation so that no power of virtue, even if it existed, could ever redeem it. Incidentally, here is part of the explanation for Hamlet taking his time to avenge this father. Dishonesty has seeped so deep into the fibres of our being that we only deceive when we profess love. "I am myself indifferent honest".

Hamlet may no longer love Ophelia, but continues to wish her well. This flower of a girl, who, he knows, is being sought to be drawn by her intriguing father into the fetid air of the court, evokes his concern and compassion. The thought of her arouses his protective instincts. He would like her to get out of the sty. He would want her to escape from the fell influences that would blight her. The human stock has become so degenerate that if she marries, she can only breed sinners. Hence, "get thee to a nunnery"

Dover Wilson would have us believe that Shakespeare must have used the term 'nunnery' to mean a brothel. He adds that Hamlet's final speech to Ophelia in this scene confirms him in his reading that 'nunnery' stands for a house of ill-fame."Nunnery' was a cant word for a house of ill fame and that Hamlet has this meaning in mind is, I think, clear from his final speech".[5]

We shall, however, try to show that his interpretation does not fit in with the intention Shakespeare seems to have given Hamlet.

In the first 'nunnery' speech, Hamlet argues that the world being what it is, Ophelia can only breed sinners, should she marry. As for Hamlet himself, he is tolerably honest and yet he is too full of evil propensities for him to give a proper account of. Mankind is so debased and degenerate that the world of men can more justly be likened to a world of slimy worms. Therefore, 'go thy ways to a nunnery.'

In the second speech, Hamlet maintains that Ophelia, should she marry, can never avoid calumny, however chaste she may be. Therefore, she should go to a nunnery. If marry she must, she should choose a fool, for wise men know what marriage makes of them; marriage means cuckoldry.

In the final 'nunnery' speech, Hamlet focuses with bitter satire on the mainfold seductive arts that women practise. Through these they strive to seem what they are not, with the only object of imposing on men and winning their favour. These have a corrupting influence on society. There shall be no more marriages than have taken place already.

Now, going by Dover Wilson's way of interpreting, Hamlet wants Ophelia to go to a brothel. The question arises: To do what? To add to the knavery and sin of the world? To be permanently stigmatised? To be condemned to perpetual 'painting, jigging, ambling, lisping and nick-naming God's creatures'? If this be what Hamlet had intended, he would be worse than a misogynist and he simply could not be believed to have ever loved Ophelia. While forbidding Ophelia to be 'a breeder of sinners', Hamlet would hardly ever have wanted her to dally with 'sinners'.

While exhorting her to escape calumny by avoiding marriage, could he arguably have desired her to invite permanent calumny on herself by walking into a brothel? After having lashed out at the follies of women, could he, conceivably, have recomnended that she immerse herself in such iniquities in perpetuity? No doubt, he is in full flood of satiric fury and he is unsparing in his censure of both men and women, especially women. It is in this mood that he is supposed to be wishing the girl he had loved and into whose soul the canker has already entered, to descend to vice and ignominy. Indeed, arguably, her world of darkness would then match the darkness in which he feels he is enclosed. And could there be greater satisfaction for him than this?

Couldn't we, however, pause and look afresh at the situation? Even though we may sound repetitive, let us go over the arguments once again. Hamlet is positive that there shall be no more marriages because marriages would be the means of breeding sinners. It is also true that the human race is irremediably corrupt. What, then, should be the role of Ophelia? Ophelia should either marry a fool, if she must marry at all, or she should go to a nunnery. If she marries a fool, he would not know that cuckoldry is his lot. If she goes to a nunnery, meaning a brothel, it would be the end of her in every conceivable sense. And yet Hamlet repeatedly exhorts her to go to a nunnery. What does he think of her now? She is not as innocent and straight in conduct as she was before. She would not, as she used to, let Hamlet approach her and talk of love. At the same time, she would make Hamlet answerable for their breaking off. This, to put it mildly, is less than fair conduct. As we have already noted, coming as it does on the heels of Gertrude's conduct, this tortuousness, rather deviousness on the part of Ophelia, puts Hamlet off completely. Once and for all, he draws his conclusion about women. Hence the bitterness of his reproach. On the other hand, however, he can guess that Ophelia has not acted on her own; somebody is pulling the strings from behind the screen, and he is no other than Polonius. Polonius is a meddler. He makes it impossible for Ophelia to be her natural self. trusting her natural reactions. He makes spontaneity of response impossible. He is responsible for the distressing distortions that Hamlet can perceive in Ophelia. She is gruesomely twisted out of the native movement of her soul Hence Hamlet's warning:

"Let the doors be shut upon him".

(III.i 132)

And Polonius who is in hiding along with the king hears it.

Ophelia's love, if love it was (at least she implies it by her references to

Hamlet's love for her), easily 'admits' impediments', easily 'bends with the remover to remove'. She does not need 'tempests' to let her love be shaken. Her father's browbeating is enough.

Wilson Knight says: "In making women strongest in love and man in action, Shakespeare is the voice for a deep truth".[6] In the same essay he talks of the "singly purposeful heroines".[7] Unfortunately, Ophelia is a sad exception to his otherwise eminently acceptable formulation. We cannot think of Ophelia as strong in love, much less as a singly purposeful heroine.

Bradley's advocacy for Ophelia has been found quite acceptable in certain critical quarters. Thus, referring to Polonius using Ophelia as a 'decoy' and her giving her father an old letter from Hamlet as an evidence of his love, A.L. French speaks approvingly of Bradley's reading of the conduct of both the father and his daughter:

> "Polonius thinks it necessary to choose Ophelia for Hamlet and to spy on them for reasons of state: this has been his attitude all along. Bradley sees this very clearly and he also exculpates Ophelia".[6]

Bradley had said:

> "Why should she not tell her father the whole story and give him an old letter which may help to convince the king and the queen? Nay, why should she not allow herself to be used as a 'decoy' to settle the question why Hamlet is mad? It is all important that it should be settled, in order that he may be cured; all her seniors are simply and solely anxious for his welfare; and if her unkindness is the cause of his sad state, they will permit her to restore him by kindness (IIII.i. 40). Was she to refuse to play a part just because it would be painful to her to do so? I find in her joining the 'plot' (as it is absurdly called) a sign not of weakness, but of unselfishness and strength".[7]

Bradley makes three points: (1) Ophelia is convinced that Hamlet's lunacy is due to being repelled by her, (2) she is anxious to see Hamlet cured, and (3) she shows unselfishness and strength in joining the 'plot'.

One finds it pretty hard to reconcile the supposed eagerness to see Hamlet cured and the supposed unselfishness and strength with the part she actually plays. And what is that part? Ophelia talks of returning his gifts. Why? The gifts, she says have lost their perfume and worth because Hamlet has proved "unkind". Which provokes his sarcasm:

Ha, ha: are you honest?

Now, the reader knows, it is not Hamlet who has proved unkind, it is she who has. Ophelia knows it too. If it was her intention to convince the king who is eavesdropping that it is affronted love that has turned Hamlet 'mad', she should have begun by making amends for her past conduct, or she should have been advised to do so by her mentor.

Granted that Ophelia is unaware of the deeper causes of Hamlet's unrest, she or her father nevertheless should have had the sense to realise that keeping quiet about her past conduct which has supposedly caused Hamlet's madness, and her going a step further to add insult to injury by squarely blaming him and offering to return his gifts would appear altogether perverse and unforgivable. Indeed, to any normal lover, her egregious self-righteousness (she is careful to claim a 'noble mind') would appear unbearably hypocritical.

But to return to our point. Ophelia, as Hamlet sees, is being drawn to the devious ways of the Danish world. It is only the beginning of the process of contamination. She, however, still retains something of her earlier innocence and goodness and it is difficult to believe or imagine that Hamlet could have really wished a soul he had once loved with all the passion of his heart, a soul still relatively free from the vices of the world, to be thrust pitilessly into the den of vice from which there could be no return. Rather it seems more reasonable to think of Hamlet, though disenchanted and made sour, solicitously wanting her to take shelter in a safe haven where she would be away from the spreading contagion of the world. This image of Hamlet desperately wanting to save her soul from imminent peril fits in with the dramatist's over-all presentation of this tragic hero. Lamb's insight into the psychology informing Hamlet's outburst in the nunnery scene is worth glancing at as being of some relevance in this context. He maintains that the alienation that he notices in the scene is temporary and not irreconcilable, and that the emotion is not so much anger as grief, not so much hate but love counterfeiting it. "The truth is, that in all such deep affections as had subsisted between Hamlet and Ophelia, there is a stock of supererogatory love....... which in any great grief of heart,...... confers a kind of indulgence upon the grieved party to express itself, even to its heart's dearest object, in the language of temporary alienation; but it is not alienation, it is a distraction purely, and so it always makes itself to be felt by that object: it is not anger, but grief assuming the appearance of anger,-love awkwardly counterfeiting hate......."[8]

Lamb's theory of temporary alienation is not tenable because he completely overlooks Ophelia's tutored role in driving Hamlet to the point of near-complete cynicism. At the same time, however, his reading has its merit in its suggestion that Ophelia has not completely forfeited her lover's good will. Hamlet's profound cynicism is yet not entirely incompatible with a certain measure of concern for her.

Let us look at Hamlet's treatment of his mother who is sunk deep in the mire of incest. In the famous closet scene in which he speaks daggers to her but uses none, he makes her see the enormity of her sin in such stinging terms that Gertrude exclaims:

> O Hamlet, speak no more!
> Thou turn'st my eyes into my very soul;
> And there I see such black and grained spots
> As will not leave their tinct.
>
> (III.iv. 88. et. seq.)

There's no softpedialling. Rather, Hamlet goes about stripping the pretences bare with such demonic fury that Gertrude nearly breaks down:

> O, speak to me no more;
> These words like daggers enter in mine ears;
> No more, sweet Hamlet.
>
> (III.iv. 94 et. seq.)

Yet, Hamlet does not think her a lost soul. He has been trying to rouse her conscience, because he still believes she has one. He would sting her, stab her with words, and yet how passionately he points the way to her moral recovery!

> Confess yourself to heaven;
> Repent what's past; avoid what is to come.
>
> (III. iv. 149-150)

How solicitous he is of her welfare!

> Once more, good night:
> And when you are desirous to be blest,
> I'll blessing beg of you.
>
> (III. iv. 170 et. seq.)

What we have been seeking to drive at is that Hamlet is equally, if not more, solicitous of Ophelia's welfare. This is one facet of his character not often recognised or perceived. His attachment to his mother and Ophelia both of whom in their different ways are responsible for his present crisis of being and against whom he rails, triumphs over his frenzied revulsion. This paradox is germane to Shakespears's conception of Hamlet, as we see it. Hence the exhortation to Ophelia to go to a nunnery- a place beyond all contagion.

But Ophelia seems destined for premature withering.

As we noted at the outset, she is perhaps the only girl in Shakespeare to surrender abjectly to her father. Bradley dilates at length on her 'child-like nature', her 'inexperience', her 'ignorance' and 'innocence'. He even seems to be getting us solicitous bits of information about her on surmise and from outside the text that is before us. One might point out that Desdemona was no less innocent nor a Miranda. Desdemona marries a person much older than she, far removed from her in racial origin, in upbringing, complexion, appearance, and so on, and she marries him in the teeth of her senator father's peremptory opposition. Miranda, who certainly holds her nearby omnipotent father in greater awe that Ophelia her father, sees Ferdinand, a complete stranger and gets enamoured of him. Not only that. She makes no secret of her hurt feelings when Prospero butts in, treats Ferdinand rudely and places hurdles in their way. Cordelia holds her ground throwing her royal father into ungovernable rage and risking her future. Or, think of a Juliet or a Celia going their ways determinedly in the face of parental wrath.

"On this childlike nature and on Ophelia's inexperience everything depends", says Bradley. One would rather say that on her inverted will everything depends. Bradley talks of Ophelia's likely age. Miranda was only fifteen. Bradley talks of the supposed difficulty created by Hamlet who is of a higher station than Ophelia. Perdita, no less but infinitely more spirited, falls for Florizel, believing herself to be the daughter of a shepherd and knowing fully well that the young man is no less than a prince.

To quote Bradley again, "for Hamlet she has, some say, no deep love- and perhaps she is so near childhood that old affections have still the strongest hold".Now compare this sketch of Ophelia with what Ophelia has to say about herself:

> And I, of ladies most deject and wretched
> That suck'd the honey of his music vows.
>
> (III.i 155-156)

It is a little difficult to believe that Shakespeare is here painting the picture of a child. Such are not the syllables in which a girl awkwardly close to her childhood speaks about her lover's passion and her reception of it. The words Ophelia uses have unquestionably the accent of an adult and so has the following speech evidencing a maturity of perception and a felicitous precision of image-making:

O, what a noble mind is here o'erthrown!
The courtier's, soldier's, scholar's eye, tongue, sword;
The expectancy and rose of the fair state,
The glass of fashion and the mould of form,
The' observ'd of all observers-quite, quite down!

(III.i. 150 et. seq.)

Shakespeare's fastidious discernment in allowing words to his men and women is universally acknowledged. He ever takes care of the fitness of words in terms of station, age, temperament and situation. Ophelia must have set her eyes upon the "observed of all obervers" and sucked "the honey of his music vows", more than once. And thus love grew. Nevertheless, she is pathetically inapt in translating that love with decision and to their mutual good. She is little more than a puppet, completely lacking even a semblance of the compulsive instinct for assertion, whether in words or otherwise, an essential property of Shakespeare's women.

And this is a puzzle and calls for a critical look.

Ophelia's death following her madness is of course attributable to frustration in love and her father's death which remained wrapped in mystery. Hamlet's frenzied reaction which she believed to have stemmed from her tutored refusal to encourage his overtures but which she did nothing sensible to assuage did affect her in no small way:

O, woe is me
T'have seen what I seen, see what I see;

(III.i. 160)

As a Shakespearian woman she should have been able to forestall the situation. But, unfortunately, she herself contributes in no small measure to the frustration that eventually breaks her heart.

T.S. Eliot makes Hamlet responsible for the death of Ophelia, among others:

"Hamlet, who has made a pretty considerable mess of things, and occasioned the death of at least three innocent people and two more insignificant ones....."9

In the perspective of our analysis of Ophelia's actions, one is rather inclined to suggest that it is she who has made a "pretty considerable mess of things". But, perhaps, even more than her lamentable docility or pliancy, it is the dread and pervasive pollution of the Danish Court that the accounts for Ophelia's disintegration and death. The grimly corrosive spirit of evil Hamlet can and does resist for a commendable while mustering his inner resources. Ophelia never even woke up to it while it went on working imperceptibly on her will and faculties, dulling them and effecting a kind of docility or distortion which made impossible an alignment with Hamlet. She aided the evil unwittingly by refusing him what she had owed him. Nevertheless, Hamlet, as we have seen, would have Ophelia save her soul.

As for Polonius's death, it needs to be pointed out that whatever the Danish Court may have thought of the procedure ("Modern critics never say how, given the situation, they think the Danish Court should have behaved towards Hamlet. I think Shakespeare showed them as behaving with reasonable good sense and decency according to their pretty limited lights"[10]) Hamlet repeatedly found him pretty insufferable. It is important to remember that Shakespeare makes Polonius hear what Hamlet thinks of him. ("Let the door be shut upon him, that he may play the fool nowhere but in's own house").

> That Polonius is an intruder, Hamlets has hinted more than once to his very face. In Act III Sc. III Polonius drives him to the very limits of exasperation. Hamlet knows that Ophelia's cooling off is her father's work. To prove his worth and indispensability to the king, Polonius has known no rest, cutting endless capers. What with his suggestions for spying and his actual involvement in them and thus getting in Hamlet's way to the latter's annoyance and anger, he has clearly been tempting his fate. His eavesdropping when Hamlet means to be alone with Gertrude constitutes a gross violation of the sanctity of the mother son relationship. The compulsive eavesdropper has to pay the penalty sooner or later. And even though Polonivs's death was not quite intended and was thus accidental, who can forget that he has been at it rather too often? The officious and self-important counsellor is responsible for his own undoing. Hamlet is just an instrument and he says as much ('but Heaven has pleas'd it so'.)
>
> To return to Ophelia. Her disability seems to be organically related to the ruling spirit of her milieu. The world of Hamlet is such that it constricts, dispirits, demoralises; that is, it saps one's energy and will in some mysterious way or other. Francisco is 'sick at heart'. The 'stoic' Horatio says that he is only a 'piece' of himself. Both Marcellus and Horatio are less than themselves when they try to restrain Hamlet from going out to meet the beckoning Ghost. Marcellus feels that 'something is rotten in the state of Denmark'. Hamlet sees the time as out of joint.Later, in his encounter with Guildenstern and Rosencrantz he makes a sort of confession which rings true;

'......... this goodly frame, the earth,seems to me a sterile promontory; this most excellent canopy, the air, look you this o' erhanging firmament ...... why, it appeareth no other thing to me than a foul and pestilent congregation of vapour.......'

(II.ii 296 et seq.)

This demoralising sense of 'sterility' and of being enclosed and stifled in a 'pestilent congregration of vapours' is a recurrent dramatic suggestion which is manipulated dexterously to create the essential and circumambient atmosphere of the world of the play. In such a world, one does not look for the usual throb of life, for the spontaneous, lusty gestures of the soul in the grip of the life-urge. In fact, the life-urge does not exist. As Hamlet expresses himself in his first soliloquy:

How weary, stale, flat and unprofitable
Seem to me all the uses of this world!
Fie on't; Ah, fie! 'tis an unweeded garden,
That grows to seed; things rank and gross in nature
Possess it merely.

(I.ii 133 et. seq.)

This psychology owes its origin to the keen perception of a contagion emanating from the Court and taking a dreadfully debilitating hold of things which explains a lack of any incentive for striving. Ophelia is stricken and debilitated without her knowing it. In fact, her tragedy is truly explainable only in terms of the foul miasma of the court which proves fatel for herself-expression and self-fulfilment. A coercive authority frigthtfully out to stifle free expression and dragoon potentially recalcitrant forces into obedience and conformity presides over the disablement and death of Ophelia who could have linked up meaningfully with Hamlet in less murky circumstances. Ophelia wilting and withering in her prime is thus best seen as indispensable to the dramatisation of the evil from which issues the miasma overhanging the world of Hamlet. Shakespeare's tragic instinct works deeper than ensuring the mundane gratification which Johnson, as the quotation at the beginning of the essay makes clear, would seek from the play and which, according to him, would consist, among other things, in seeing Claudius destroyed and Ophelia kept alive.

REFERENCES:-

1. *Shakespeare Criticism:* A Selection 1623-1840, ed. D. Nichol Smith (World's Classic) p. 199
2. Ibid p.122

3. *Form and Meaning in Drama*. Kitto, 1960 p. 279.
4. Ibid 279.
5. *Hamlet, The New Shakespeare*, C.U.P., 1969. p. 193
6. 'The Shakespearian Integrity' in *Shakespeare Criticism* (1935-1960) ed. Anne Ridler, O.U.P., 1970, p. 178.
7. Ibid p. 177.
8. *Shakespeare and the Critics*, 1972, p. 32.
9. *Shakespearean Tragedy*, p.131.
10. *Shakespeare Criticism* 1623-1840, ed. D.N. Smith, O.V.P., 1958
11. *'Shakespeare and the Stocism of Seneca'* in *Shakespeare Citicism*, 1919-1935, ed. Anne Classics 1956, p.216 Riddler O.V.P., (World's)Classics 1956, p.216
12. *Shakespeare and the Critics*, A.L. French, p.33.

OPHELIA AND THE TRAGIC DESIGN

There appears to be a kind of family resemblance between Dickens's Gradrind and Shakespeare's Polonius in spite of the vast difference in station and function separating them. One takes his stubborn, self-deluding stand on 'facts', the other on his own brand of experience, Neither of them can ever conceive of being proved wrong. Both believe in teaching and infallibly at that. Mr. Gradgrind has his own school where his daughter, like every other pupil, is forced into the straight jacket of his system and Polonius is ever teaching his daughter to conform in order to be worthy of his status and honour.

> Marry, I'll teach you.
>
> (I.iii.104)

Contemplating the sad fate of Ophelia one may not perhaps be accused of being overly fanciful to be listening to the following bit of conversation between father and daughter, assuming them to have lived long enough for the occasion.

> 'I never knew you were unhappy, my child'. 'Father, I always knew it. In this strife I have almost repulsed and crushed my better angel into a demon. What I have learnt has left me doubting, misbelieving, despising, regretting what I have not learned, and my dismal recourse has been to think that life would soon go by, and nothing in it could be worth the pain and trouble of a contest'.[1]

As in the other great plays of Shakespeare, there is in *Hamlet* too, a deft and pervasive exploitation of similitudes and *antitheses*. Hamlet's revenge motive glances at those of Leartes and Fortinbras. His insecurity (he is 'dreadfully attended') connects ironically with Claudius's. His 'secret' ("There's something in his soul/O'er which his melancholy sits on brood") again calls attention to that of Claudius. Ophelia's madness looks back at the feigned madness of Hamlet and so on.

Now the design of the play is such that if the reality of insanity invites reference to the simulation of it, the suicidal obedience to a parent calls for a close look at the opposite instance of dour selfassertion in the face of parental injunction to the contrary. It is a paradox that Hamlet and Ophelia inhabit the same world and yet do not. An understanding of this paradox would seem to hold a key to an understanding of the play, or at least of much of what it is about. In the dramatist's conception of their functions, they are as far apart from each other as any two persons who had once been drawn towards each other could possibly be. And in their diametrically opposed ways, they call attention to the same world which is the focus of the play, and which, under the garb of civility, poses an absolute menace to freedom and choice, -- that is, to man's status as man. This world expects conformity to its insidious ways and is gloweringly hostile to and destructive of everything truly human - whether it is a warm, fresh impulse towards union or an innate sense of values resulting in some action or attitude. By an unrelenting pursuit of his chosen path, Hamlet insistently rivets our attention on to a world of appalling evil, while the pathetic collapse and disintegration of Ophelia's mind serves to electrify our consciousness of the same soul-destroying evil.

In Act I Scene II when Hamlet makes his first appearance with all his singularity, cutting an ominous figure, Gertrude expresses her disapproval of his continued mourning:

> Good Hamlet, cast thy nighted colour off,
> And let thine eye look like a friend on Denmark.
>
> (68-69)

And Claudius joins her in censuring his conduct:

> .... to persever
> In obstinate condolement is a course
> Of impious stubbornness.
>
> (92 et seq)

Finally, Hamlet promises obedience when Gertrude implores him not to go back to Wittenberg.

> I shall in all my best obey you, madam.
>
> (120)

But we know what Hamlet means by this promise, for his mistrust of them is immeasurable. And when the Ghost enters his world to make the horrid revelation, he knows for certain what to think of the present king and his queen. To the Ghost's exhortation that his command be remembered, Hamlet's answer is that he will have nothing else to remember.

> And thy commandment all alone shall live
> Within the book and volume of my brain,
> Unmix'd with baser matter.

(I.V 102 et seq.)

Naturally, his earlier promise to their majesties to obey them goes with 'baser matter'. Indeed, he couldn't have meant to obey that 'most pernicious woman' and that 'smiling, damned villain'.

He soon decides to set in motion his scheme of dealing with them, choosing his own mode of action. To his mother gone perverse he will 'speak daggers' so as to make her glimpse the depths of inequity to which she has fallen; he will out-wit and out-manoeuver the murderer-king.

This refusal to toe the line throws into sharp relief Ophelia's abject surrender.

Laertes is the first to issue chilling prescriptions to Ophelia. He richly anticipates his father in using the language of admonition and command. He all too easily puts on the mentor. He has a closed and opaque mind which considers itself already stocked with all the experience of the world and the benefits gained therefrom. So that he speaks with an air of certitude undisturbed by any foul breath of doubt. This certitude amounts to a kind of brazen coarseness barren of that enlightened sensibility which is able to recognise and sympathise with another point of view and which, thus, is alive to the possibility of a variety of experience, equally authentic. With rank insensitivity he holds forth on the inadvisability, even the impropriety of Ophelia going about with Hamlet whom he claims to have read through and through.

> For Hamlet, and the trifling of his favour,
> Hold it a fashion and a toy in blood;
> A violet in the youth of primy nature,
> Forward not permanent, sweet not lasting,
> The perfume and suppliance of a minute;
> No more.

(I. iii. 5 et seq)

He ends his harangue with the injunction:

> Be wary, then; best safety lies in fear.

(I. iii. 43)

How about his father?

Life stands arrested and petrified for Polonius who has neatly summed it up in his maxims. Not only has he reduced it once and for all to his own set terms and categories; he would expect, even command individual lives to conform to and fit into them. An individual exploration of life is something he does not understand and frowns upon. He orders the lives of his children to suit his ideas of 'policy' and 'practice'. With Laertes who is already his father in the making, he has no problems. Ophelia calls for a little disciplining. Her goings on with Hamlet offend his sense of propriety and decorum. It is no wonder, therefore, that he is distinctly positive and authoritarian in his pronouncements.

> Do not believe his vows; for they are brokers.
>
> (I. iii. 127)

Finally, he warns her against slandering any of her 'idle' moments by giving audience to Hamlet:

> Look to't, I charge you. (I. iii. 135)

To which Ophelia capitulates:

> I shall obey, my Lord. (I. iii 136)

Indeed, she obeys in every movement of hers. She disobeys her heart and obeys her tyrant-mentors. It was much too tame, the way she sought to speak for Hamlet and his love.

Completely brow-beaten and bullied she will henceforth do her father's bidding and be a good child. (Has not Kitto said that there is nothing wrong in her obeying her 'wise' father?[2]) She will cease to be herself and play dictated roles. Much to the glee and gratification of her father, she will prevaricate, simulate grievances and thus shock Hamlet into those ungovernable tempests of outraged feelings.

By her acts of compliance, she remains within the confines of the Court and loses the needed opportunity of being with Hamlet and entering his world. This staying put in the slimy, make-believe world of the Court debars her from the knowledge she would have possessed if only she had acted courageously. Hamlet has knowledge, besides his intuitions, which enable him to look at the Court in the true perspective. And so he assails it after his fashion. Ophelia chooses to remain a prisoner and thus chooses to remain ignorant. She remains benighted and does not wake up to the fact that the Court of which her father is a valued member is rotten at its core, that it nurtures incest and fratricide, that the whole of Denmark has become a prison under its fear-some and jealous aegis. Denmark is a prison, says Hamlet to Rosencrantz and Guildenstern. His percepience enables him to see the reality of the situation and he has the resources of his spirit to resist being a docile inmate of this prison. Ophelia's unawareness is her imprisonment, for unawareness is no magic spell against her virtual confinement and strangulation. It is a fell dispensation reminiscent of that of Satan and his peers, intent on hoodwinking the unwary and presenting falsehood as truth using deceit. Ophelia does not know that her 'wise' father holds his pride of place in the Court because of his having ingratiated himself with the king by assenting and securing the assent of the rest of the nobility to his dubious succession to the throne.

This Court reminds one of the latter-day despotic regimes, especially the Nazi dispensation, largely ignorant but ruthless, intolerant of the slightest signs of non-conformity and deviation. It is no respector of means, sets friends spying upon friends, desecrates such private relationships as between mother and son and between those whom the mutuality of yearning has brought together. It considers nothing too sacred, spurning private values to consolidate and enlarge its ungodly domain. Let us listen to Polonius and Claudius. The passages cited below suggest a morbid zest for and glee in eavesdropping which is another name for ribald intrusion.

Polonius. At such a time I'll loose my daughter to him.
Be you and I behind an arras then;
Mark the encounter:

(II. ii. 161 et. seq)

Claudius. Sweet Gertrude, leave us too;
For we have closely sent for Hamlet hither,
That he, as 'twere by accident may here affront Ophelia:
Her father and myself, - lawful espials -
Will so bestow ourselves that, seeing unseen,
We may of their encounter frankly judge;

(III. i 28 et. seq)

Polonius. Ophelia, walk you here. Gracious, so please you
We will bestow ourselves.

(III. i 43-44)

Polonius. My Lord, do as you please;
But if you hold it fit, after the play

Let his queen mother all alone entreat him;
To show his grief!
Let her be round with him,
And I'll be plac'd so please you, in the ear
Of all their conference.

(III. i 180 et. seq)

Polonius. 'He will come straight. Look you lay home to him;
Tell him his pranks have been too broad to bear with,
And that your Grace hath screen'd and stood between
Much heat and him. I'll silence me even here.

(III. iv. 1 et. seq)

There is an inescapable note of unconscious irony in Polonius urging the queen to be 'round' with Hamlet and going to 'silence' himself in his chosen hiding place, for in the event it is Halmet who gets round with his mother, and in a way, with Polonius himself who, thanks to that pass through the arras, does not live to find himself silenced for ever.

When Polonius gets slain, Ophelia is not told of the circumstances of his death. This is characteristic of the set pattern of functioning of the Court which has studiedly kept her in the dark about whatever has been happening. She has been kept a mere child, though it is clear she is past the stage of childhood, having felt and recognised the impulses of love for a young man whose image she has fondly entertained. She is discerning enough to characterise Hamlet's overtures as honourable. Further, she expresses the hope that Laertes who has so officiously warned her against being too liberal with Hamlet will not himself choose 'the primrose path of dalliance' during his stay abroad. But her family environment, smacking of the Court atmosphere, will not let her come to a full realisation of her potential. It has kept her mentally stunted and dwarfed. On the other hand, she cannot escape her own share of responsibility for the sad pass she is in, for she has never tried to pull herself together, but has meekly given in.

The unexplained death of her father causes her heart-break leading to the dissolution of her mind. Ophelia, girt round with an infirmity of will, hurtles down pretty fast towards self-oblivion and extinction. She is, as Claudius says, 'divided from herself and her fair judgement'. One may notice in passing that Ophelia never gave evidence of 'fair judgement' which, if listened to, would have bid her go a different way. As we have said, Polonius's death must have been the immediate cause of her mental break-down. However, as we have also pointed out, the old man had been tempting his fate by his eavesdropping itch making him spy with irrepressible and obnoxious gusto.

Whatever one may say about a high Minister of State having "the right to spy and use suspect means to achieve a worth while end", the audience feels quite rightly that Polonius does not quite belong to the arras. "Even the moralistic critic derives some satisfaction in seeing Polonius hoist with his own petard". "To society and even to the law, the devious means are repugnant, however moral the intention. A deeply engrained 'folk morality'.......cherishes openness, candour and directness; we realise that no man is safe and no life secure in an atmosphere of mutual suspicion and distrust".[3]

It is noteworthy that Hamlet, who is our interpreter of the moral action of the play, does not blame himself too much for the deed.

> Queen. O, what a rash and bloody deed is this!
> Hamlet. A bloody deed! -- almost as bad, good mother,
> As kill a king and marry with his brother.

(III. iv. 27 et. seq)

And then turning to Polonius lying dead, he comments:

> Thou wretched, rash, intruding fool, farewell!
> ....
> Thou find'st to be too busy is some danger

(III. iv. 31 et. seq)

Polonius's code of ethics was that of the Court. The intimidated and enfeebled Ophelia is the hapless victim of that code of ethics. Since she had clung on to Polonius, his exit from the scene robs her of her moorings. She was, as we have noted, kept ignorant and repressed. Now the stifling sense of ignorance and repression, both of which have been forced on her by the Establishment, claims its due.

In her distraction, she makes wild, vague and ignorant surmises. Being in a state of nescience, she can only blunder in her guesses, as the populace does in such circumstances. It is not without significance that her delirious mumblings and inscrutable gestures feed fat the many unwholesome rumours that are afloat among the public.

Gent. She speaks much of her father; says she hears
> There's tricks i 'th' world, and hems, and beats her heart;
> Spurns enviously at straws; speaks things in doubt,
> That carry but half sense. Her speech is nothing.
> Yet the unshaped use of it doth move.
> The hearers to collection; they yawn at it.
> And botch the words up fit to their own thoughts;

Which, as her winks and nods, and gestures yield them,
Indeed would make one think there might be thought.
....
'Twere good she were spoken with; for she may strew
Dangerous conjectures in ill-breeding minds.

(IV. v 4 et. seq)

Thus, her winks and nods and gestures are grist to the public mill spawning wild and dangerous speculations. It is an irony that after having been an unwitting prisoner of the world of civility, she has now unwitting by turned out to be its enemy. In her madness she inspires the populace in their game of darting shafts of suspicion at the Court. Her repression which has fed on the very pith of her life is attested by the snatches of her songs.

One may perhaps justifiably ask the question: Why is Claudius in such a hurry to hush up the murder? Why does he 'inter' Polonius's body 'in hugger-mugger'? The answer is not far to seek. He is sorely perplexed and afraid. The situation is proving nearly too much for him to keep in control. It looks as though it will get out of hand. He has more than one skeleton in the cup-board. He does not bring himself to talk openly of Polonius's murder. Were he to do so, he would have to do more explaining than he is prepared to or capable of. His credibility is almost wholly in question. He is all too aware of the circumstances in which Polonius lost his life. It is not as though he had nothing to do with them. Discretion forbids him to lay bare the facts of the case. His guilt is much too palpable. Even as it is, his name has not been spared by the suspicious public. To declare that Hamlet is the murderer might make matters even worse for him. He knows, as he confides to Gertrude, that the public tongue-

Like to a murd' ring piece, in many places
Gives me superfluous death.

(IV. v. 91)

More than Hamlet, it is he who is the culprit. The guilt is very much on his conscience.

When Hamlet bludgeoned Ophelia in his satiric fury on the depravities of the female world, she thought he had lost his reason. Indeed, his reason was on the point of over-turning. He kept his grip over it with much difficulty by drawing upon the hidden resources of his being. Ophelia now actually loses her reason 'without the which we are pictures or mere beasts', for she has never learnt to try the resources of her being which, therefore, cannot come to her rescue. In fact, what strikes one continually and forcefully through out the play is the way Hamlet faces up to the murderous situation, holding undimmed the vision that has nourished him and keeps his enemy at bay by calling forth his moral vigour so as to be able to accomplish his supernaturally imposed task. Ophelia's slender hold on her mind and will, and her all too easy capitulation leading to her sad end seems distinctly designed to set off, by contrast, the role of Hamlet.

Because of the mysterious death of Polonius and Hamlet's departure from the scene (mysterious to the public), an increasing sense of uncertainty has overtaken the public mind which has turned restive to Claudius's discomfort and dismay. A hush-hush pervades the entire body-politic. Claudius's credentials suffer a set-back, his authority can no longer be taken for granted. The masked murderer is not only ill at ease but in a state of mortal terror. His soul is gripped by panic. Polonius's exit has brought home to him how badly his calculations have gone awry and how he has nearly been tripped by the course of events. The harried Claudius at first tries to avert a crisis by putting the best face on the situation:

> Come, Gertrude, we'll call up our wisest friends;
> And let them know both what we mean to do
> And what's untimely done....
>
> (IV. i)

Ophelia in the meantime has gone mad, letting loose suspicious rumours all over the state. People start suspecting foul play on the part of the king. Laertes is back home crazily feeding on the uncontrollable popular suspicion.

> O Gertrude, Gertrude!
> When sorrows come, they come not single spies,
> But in battalions!
>
> (IV. v. 74-75)

This speech points to the utter desperation of the king, allwhose resources have been harnessed to contain the situation to no effect. That his authority is a mere shambles becomes clear from what the Gentleman says.

> Save yourself, my Lord:
> The ocean, overpeering of his list,
> Eats not the flats with more impitious haste
> Than young Laertes, in a riotous head,

O' erbears your officers. The rabble call him lord;
And, as the world were now but to begin,
Antiquity forgot, custom not known,
The ratifiers and props of every word,
They cry, 'Choose we; Laertes shall be king'.
Caps, hands, and tongues, applaud it to the clouds,
'Laertes shallbe king, Laertes king'.

(IV. v. 95 et. seq)

The situation invites some comparison with that in *Macbeth* where the killings and tyranny of the usurper have eventually led to a complete alienation of the people among whom rebellious suspicions are rife:

Foul whisp' rings are abroad. Unnatural deeds
Do breed unnatural troubles.....

(V. i. 69-70 et. seq)

Macbeth himself gives tragic expression to his sense of the travesty of his authority:

Seyton!—I am sick at heart
When I behold—Seyton, I say!—This push
Will cheer me ever, or disseat me now.
I have liv'd long enough:......
Curses not loud but deep, mouth-honour, breath,
Which the poor heart would fain deny, and dare not.

(V. ii. 20 et. seq)

One is aware of the essential difference in Shakespeare's conception of Macbeth and Claudius, the latter being entirely without the tragic grandeur of the former. One is further aware that the crisis for Claudius on which we have been dwelling is of a passing character. The point in making this comparison is to focus in each play on the ruler's forfeiture of public confidence, the erosion of his authority, on the onrush of a kind of darkness and chaos and turmoil in the kingdom which in the case of *Hamlet* is paralleled by the turmoil in Ophelia's mind completely shattering it. The insurrection in the state is paralleled by the insurrection in Ophelia's mind. They are dramatically brought together. It is indeed difficult to escape the fact that the popular insurrection led by Laertes is immediately preceded by Ophelia shown in her distraction and going about singing her mad songs. The dramatic point obviously is that both the insurrections are ascribable to the same cause - suspicion of trickery on the part of the king. The deep suspicion that the king is a masked villain who is responsible, in some way, for the death of Polonius and the absence of Hamlet from the scene, has overturned Ophelia's mind, as it has sparked off the popular revolt in favour of Laertes. It is significant that when Laertes asks Claudius why he did not proceed against Hamlet, the latter gives two reasons for not doing so: first, the queen "lives almost by his (Hamlet's) looks" and he dared not alienate her by proceeding against him; and secondly, he is such a darling of the people

> Who, dipping all his faults in their affection,
> Would like the spring that turneth wood to stone,
> Convert his gyves to graces;
>
> (IV. vii. 19 et. seq)

Hamlet is too firmly lodged in the affections of the people who are by the same token only too quick to point their fingers at Claudius. This is attested by the insurrection we have dwelt upon above. The total impression of the relevant scenes easily lends itself to seeing Claudius as the criminal. In fact, the thrust of the entire dramatic movement in this context is to drive home the essential criminality of the king. It is noteworthy that Polonius's death serves to create a trauma for the king when Hamlet dismisses the incident almost with a shrug of his shoulder. The outer, incidental fact of Hamlet killing Polonius is made the dramatic means of directing attention to something deeper, - the primal, covert source of intrigue and murder which, coupled with incest, are seated in the heart of the world that the play is about.

Ophelia's madness and death are thus dramatically meant to be seen as a tribute to the Minotaur of the Danish Court over which the false and scheming Claudius presides. Her splintered songs are symbolic of her splintered world, of the rape of her mind. Indeed, her songs are terrifying as revelatory of her befouled and broken self and as pointing to the foul forces that worked corrosively on her, preventing her from blossoming and being her full and free self.

The sad fate of Ophelia serves to define the world of enormous evil of which she is a victim in truly Blakean terms. She came to find herself stifled amid the fatal world of experience to which no sooner had she woken up than she started to break inwardly and went to pieces. It is not without significance that Ophelia applies the characteristically Blakean image of the tyrant-hypocrite to Laertes who has just cautioned her against Hamlet's advances:

I shall be effect of this good lesson keep
As watchman to my heart. But, good my brother,
Do not, *as some ungracious pastors do,*
Show me the steep and thorny way to heaven,
Whiles, like a puff'd and reckless libertine,
Himself the primrose path of dalliance treads
And recks not his own rede.

(italics added I. iii. 45 et. seq)

Polonius and Laertes habitually use the prescriptive and prohibitory idiom, the language of icy imperatives, reminding us of Blake's 'The Garden of Love' which provides a singularly apt analogy to the atmosphere in which Ophelia wilts and withers. All spontaneity choked and smothered, and, intimidated by the language of dont's - 'Thou shalt not', the child suffers a heart-break seeing its cherished garden of love disappear giving place to a chapel (bearing on its door chilling injunctions) and to graves and tombstones with demonic social elders going round sadistically "binding with briars my joy and desires".

The child's experience is indeed a perfect analogue to Ophelia's. Were she ever to wake up to the reality when she was in command of her reason, she would cry out as the Earth does in Blake:

Break this heavy chain
That does freeze my bones around.

Ophelia's world, too, is one where

Love seeketh only self to please,
To bind another to its delight,
Joys in another's loss of ease
And builds a Hell in Heaven's despite.

She is the sick rose of Blake destroyed by the "invisible worm/That flies in the night/In the howling storm". She has been desecrated and ruined by the agents of darkness.

The queen's funeral speech in which the vision of 'bride-bed' turns into the numb despair of the grave enacts the same relentless mode of thought that metamorphoses in Blake's *London* the marriage-bed into the 'marriage-hearse':

I thought thy bride-bed to have deck'd sweet maid,
And not have strew'd thy grave.

(V. i. 238-39)

Her recital of the circumstances of Ophelia's drowning is a telling example of the realising power of language. It performs more than one function. It is a visualisation not only of the manner of Ophelia's death but also of her mode of life. Ophelia had cartainly meant to be with Hamlet to unite with him and be his wife - a quite reasonable proposition for a girl of her position - a proposition which, however, could not even come close to being translated into reality, thanks considerably to her timid compliance with the contrary wishes of her family. The lack of determination marking her proceeding and the deflection from her path due to hostile environment seem reflected in the image of her 'clambering' to hang her 'coronet weeds' on the 'pendant bough' when 'an envious sliver broke' causing her to fall into the 'weeping brook'. The malicious sliver may be seen to correspond to the malicious family which made it impossible for her to gain a secure foothold in life and which thus paved the way to her dislocation and death. This process of slipping away from her attempts at relating herself to life is indeed aptly conveyed in the image discussed. The family which she was induced to trust as the only place from which would come her much-needed support and guidance proves only to be a semblance of refuge not unlike the garments which sustaining her for a while, eventually

> Pull'd the poor wretch from her melodious lay
> To muddy death.
>
> (IV. vii 183)

The short life that she lived had all the suggestion of unreality about it. She was separated from herself. The dichotomy between her anguished inner self and the external ritual of existence apparently insensible of the psychic desolation, the cruel chasm between the facade and the reality is powerfully captured in the beautiful-grotesque image:

> Her clothes spread wide;
> And, mermaid-like, while they bore her up:
> Which time she chanted snatches of old lauds,
> As one incapable of her own distress,
> Or like a creature native and indued
> Unto that element.
>
> (IV. vii. 176 et. seq)

It is an unutterably sad picture of the miming exterior having no commerce with the wounded and grieving inner self. This is but the prelude to dissolution and death. In fact, her disengagement from Hamlet was prognostic of death, for it was the expression of her death-wish as opposed to her will to live. Stretching the suggestion of the last two lines of the passage quoted above, one might say that she, even when alive, had belonged more to 'that element' than to earth, more to death than to life.

Ophelia's pathetic stasis and obliteration are a means of clarifying the moral vision of the play. No doubt she dies in a state of obedience. But she had done something decisive before her passing to set in motion the process of disintegration of the regime that had caused her inanity. In the insensibility of her dementia she is the cause of disaffection and disobedience in the minds of Claudius's subjects who break into rebellion for however short a while. And her brother Laertes who, barring a short-lived rebellion, has been in league with the king to the point of plotting against Hamlet's life ends up disowning Claudius,bearing testimony against him, and befriending Hamlet. The irony is complete and devastating. And it is germane to the essential scheme of the play.

References:-

1. Gradgrind and Louisa in *Hard Times*, Book the Second, Chapter XII.
2. *Form and Meaning in Drama*, 1960, p.279.
3. 'Historical Criticism and The Interpretation of Shakespeare' Robert Ornstein in *Approaches to Shakespeare*, ed. Norman Rabkin, Mc. Graw-Hill, 1964, pp. 177-178.

SAMSON AGONISTES : SPIRIT AND TECHNIQUE

So rose the Danite strong,
Herculean Samson, from the harlot-lap
Of Philistean Dalilah, and waked
Shorn of his strength.

Paradise Lost, Bk. ix

The reference to Samson in these lines is significant for it not only shows Milton's awareness of a certain parallelism between Adam's folly and that of Samson, but points to his imaginative sensibility being deeply affected even at the time of writing *Paradise Lost* (going by the generally accepted chronology according to which *Paradise Lost* is prior to both *Paradise Regained* and *Samson Agonistes)* by the image of 'Herculean Samson' reduced to impotence for transgression brought about by an effeminate surrender to female importunity. In fact, the theme of *Samson Agonistes* substantially looks back to *Paradise Lost* with its disobedience, fall, contrition and promise of final recovery. At the same time *Samson Agonistes* re-enacts the main feature of *Paradise Regained*, for corresponding to the contrast between Adam's weak surrender to Eve in *Paradise Lost* and Christ's conquest of temptations in *Paradise Regained*, there is, within the single movement of *Samson Agonistes*, the sharp contrast between Samson's earlier surrender to Delilah and his later triumph over sore temptations.

Into *Samson Agonistes* the Milton of both *Paradise Lost* and *Paradise Regained* enters implacably with the same burning consciousness of a sacred covenant between man and God (a consciousness that marks out Milton the man and Milton the poet as it does hardly any other English poet of comparable stature), and of that convenant being outrageously breached by erring man, who, hitherto a picture of confident and ebullient strength and now an image of self-accusation and self-laceration, suffers from an ineradicable feeling of alienation.

Samson Agonistes being a tragedy in the classical mould has often been noticed and commented on. Thus George Steiner says: 'It is through *Samson Agonistes*, more readily perhaps than through archaeology and classical scholarship, that we glimpse the lost totality of Greek drama.'[1] And William P. Parker observes: '*Samson Agonistes* is "Greek" in the sense that a tragedy written in the days of Aristotle might have been.... Because the English Poet had intellectual or artistic affinities with each of his three models, he wrote—not as an imitator of one of them, or two—but as a great successor of all three.'[2] While the conspicuous Hellenic form of the work legitimately elicits such critical comments as quoted above, it is not as often recognized that the distinctive tone of it is Puritan and not Greek. The sense of having committed a sin in conscious violation of a divine injunction, clearly understood and devoutly accepted, a sin giving rise to a sense of pollution or desecration is built into the work. The consequent feeling of being a lapsed soul is central to the ruling temper of the play as we see it. As we shall try to demonstrate, the unrelenting sternness of this puritan temper is manifest all-through the work. The spirit of exclusion in which the fearsome sternness of temper expresses itself characterises not only the dramatic thrust of the protagonist's character but also the essential dramatic mechanism as we see it. Samson is self-flagellating; he is 'self-severe' and 'implacable', and this is because from an overwhelming puritan sense of pollution he is resolved to deny or exclude some element as a means of restoration. To restore himself to himself, he has to exclude a part of himself from his total being; he has to exclude his baser from his nobler self, even as he has to exclude the rest of the world. And a similar spirit of exclusion will be seen as marking out a significant dramatic device that one can see at work right from the beginning to the end.

The basic theme of *Samson Agonistes* can be said to be the fallen, forsaken and punished man's laboured search for his God from the Slough of Despond to the Celestial City through Doubting Castle. Samson passes and repasses through the whole complex gamut of feelings and attitudes between 'a sense of Heaven's desertion' and a lingering hope for 'His final pardon'. Indeed, most of the action of *Samson Agonistes* would seem to be held in a state of soul-tearing tension between these two poles of abysmal despair and tremulous hope. The experience this tension mirrors is characteristic of early Christianity and Puritanism. It not only recalls but throws into sharp relief the Augustinian concepts of *privatio Dei* (the turning away from God, the highest Good, to the perishable world), *contemptus mundi* (contempt of the world) and *amor Dei* (love of God). At the same time it would seem, at least in some measure, to anticipate for all temperamental, situational and theological differences, Hopkins's tortured sensibilities: '...and why must in Disappointment all I endeavour end?/...O thou lord of life, send my roots rain.' And here is Samson's anguished cry:

Why was my breeding ordered and prescribed
As of a person separate to God,
Designed for great exploits, if I must die
Betrayed, captived, and both my eyes put out..

Milton's Puritan vision of ultimate human worth and the fulfilment of human destiny is understandably awesome, while the human worth glimpsed and credited is put, again understandably, to its grimmest test. And it is indeed significant that to communicate this momentous vision, he has recourse to the form of Greek tragedy; significant because it illustrates a peculiar compatibility between Milton's Puritan vision and the Greek form, between the appeal of Hellenic and of Hebrew influences. As observed by Hutchinson: 'If the form and style are Greek, the spirit is Hebraic and reflects Milton's Puritan mind.'[3] His Puritan mind could not but adore the form of Greek tragedy with its ruthless, inflexible single aim of advancing the action undeflected by any wayside interest.

The artist in Milton takes hold of his sexual, ethical and religious attitudes (as displayed in *Paradise Lost*), fuses them together and finally transfigures them into a compelling work of art in the classic mould. Something of a Philoctetes and a Prometheus, Samson recalls a good deal of *Oedipus at Colonus* . A Philoctetes in his wretchedness and squalor, a Prometheus in his stubborn definance of evil, he comes pretty close to Oedipus in his blindness, in his self-reproach and self-questionings and finally in his vision leading to the fearsome surrender to the Divine.

What is, however, especially to the point and deserves critical notice is that in spite of these classical resemblances, Milton's protagonist remains pre-eminently the Puritan that Milton is. In the Greek conception of things, God is something alien, mysterious, unaccountable, and therefore dreaded. The Hebrew God is dreaded too, but with a difference. The sense of being chosen for merit and then forsaken for transgression in the over-all context of a personal God-man relationship, and of a responsible Providence, is not quite germane to Greek thought as it is to either Hebrew or Christian theology. The divine hostility to Prometheus or Oedipus—one with a sense of being in the right till the end, and the other rather trapped into sinning—is entirely a different matter from God's anger on account of Samson's breach of divine trust. Of his own admission, Samson consciously accepted the trust and, equally consciously, violated it. He has 'profaned/The mystery of god, given me under pledge/Of vow.' The sense of being alienated from God and of being tainted is a natural consequence of a Puritan's faith, for he is a stickler for purity, his purity consisting in a strict obedience to God's decrees which commend themselves to man's understanding and acceptance. To such a decree he has proved false. His being plagued today is consciously his own doing. Thus in his opening speech:

> What is all foretold
> Had been fulfilled but through mine own default?
> Whom have I to complain of but myself,
> Who this high gift of strength committed to me,
> In what part lodged, how easily bereft me,
> Under the seals of silence could not keep,
> But weakly to a woman must reveal it,
> O' ercome with importunity and tears?

And now to Manoa:

> Appoint not heavenly disposition, father,
> Nothing of all these evils hath befallen me
> But justly; I myself have brought them on;
> Sole author I, sole cause.

I have been false to my God; I have been false to myself; I have chosen the world in preference to God—this would seem to be the burden of his agonised cry. Thus viewed, from *Samson Agonistes* would seem to issue forth a long-drawn wail—the wail of alienation and an irrepressible spirit of urgency for setting at naught this alienation and for being restored to God's grace. The impression is inescapable that this world and all that goes with it is evil, is abominable and that what matters to the exclusion of all else is God's grace and favour to fall upon you. It is clear that 'to displease/God for the fear of man, and man prefer,/Set God behind,' is the most unforgivable sin. The road to salvation lies through contempt of the world and love of God. And this is what Augustine meant by *Contemptus mundi* and *amor Dei*. For Samson there is a two-fold call—a call from those around him and a call from beyond. Milton shows Samson dealing with these exclusive calls and wrestling with himself. And in the process he shows his vision—his vision of human worth to which we have referred previously.

Milton turns the spotlight on, the dramatises with an intensity rarely matched in English drama, the supreme human predicament in which the protagonist comes to grips with, interprets and finally fulfils the terms for divine acceptance. Here is an extraordinarily dramatic protrayal of a dilemma finally resolved in a sudden burst of illumination which can be, and is, stunning for both reader and spectator.

Samson's predicament is first hinted at by his own words:

> Retiring from the popular noise, I seek
> This unfrequented place to find some ease—
> Ease to the body some, none to the mind
> From restless thoughts....

The chorus later focuses on this predicament:

> This idol's day hath been to thee no day of rest,
> Labouring thy mind
> More than the working dav thy hands.

Samson's soul is stretched to the uttermost and the final moment has arrived. He must choose between the two—the terrestrial call and the divine; the terrestriat call is represented in the figures of Manoa, Delilah and Harapha, each in his or her way offering a false sense of security. There is, on the other hand, the divine call for going the whole hog in the face of all suffering. In the midst of suffering and faced with a seemingly endless slavery to the Philistines, Samson does at times waver in his faith, but the one thing he has firmly turned his face against is to succumb to the temptations, to seek reconciliation with his enemies. As Delilah, who employed all her wiles to bring about a change in his mind, puts it picturesquely:

> I see thou art implacable, more deaf
> To prayers than winds and seas. Yet winds to seas
> Are reconciled at length, and sea to shore:
> Thy anger, unappeasable, still rages,
> Eternal tempest never to be calmed.

Rising superior to all specious pleas for reconciliation with the soul-negating forces, to all manner to blandishments and bullyings— in other words, repudiating all earthly temptations which, to the discerning mind, point the way to the soul's ruination, the protagonist, aided by his prescience, firmly responds to the call of Providence, to the imperious summons to the supreme feat of self-sacrifice leading to self-recovery and self-fulfilment. It can be seen that just before he takes the final leap, knowledge has grown so puissant and imperious as inevitably to result in his cutting himself loose from the down-hill pull of finitude and flying out, so to speak, to merge in the bosom of the infinite.

This work which, in the opinion of T.S. Eliot, could have been a masterpiece—'The appropriateness of the subject of Samson is too obvious to expatiate upon: it was probably the one dramatic story out of which Milton could have made a masterpiece'[4]—and thus by implication was not, invites, curiously enough, some comparison with *Murder in the Cathedral.*

Before proceeding further we should like to record our awarness of the fact that Eliot's work, as distinct from Milton's which breathes the Hebraic-Puritanic spirit, is conceived in the New Testament spirit and that the two deaths dramatised are not on all fours. Samson's death is a case of self-killing which Thomas's death is not. It needs pointing out, however, that the self-killing involved in the destruction of the enemy was called for by the circumstances of the story. Even more important is the fact that the holocaust that we witness at the end of *Samson Agonistes* is not only a scriptural event, but one rendered dramatically appropriate and necessary in the context of the over-all design of the tragedy. This is what the chorus says:

> O dearly bought revenge, yet glorious!
> Living or dying thou hast fulfilled
> The work for which thou was foretold
> To Israel, and now liest victorious
> Among thy slain self-killed;
> Not willingly, but tangled in the fold
> of dire Necessity....

And the Semichorus on Samson's victims:

> So fond are mortal men,
> Fallen into wrath divine,
> As their own ruin on themselves to invite,
> Insensate left or to sense reprobate
> And with blindness internal struck.

Yet in another respect the two plays are different. Unlike Samson, Thomas harbours no sense of being guilty of any profane act, of having violated any bond or trust between himself and his God. He is not touched with any sense of pollution such as bears Samson down and makes him the prey of a complex variety of emotions thus lending a weight and a dimension not to be expected in Eliot's play.

However, what seems especially to the point while one is dwelling on the analogy between the two plays, is that the nature of Samson's end is no less providential than that of Thomas's death. Both have the conviction of being led to their acts of choice by God himself on their final day on earth. In either play the protagonist is pitted against an evil of menacing proportions and against dire temptations.

In both cases, the soul is brought to a stage-a climacteric one—where it is left to its sole self, its own resources, to negotiate a final deal with the supreme. The way of escape is left open. It remains an open proposition for the protagonist to turn away from the fearsome, flesh-negating path of choosing God in preference to the enticing prospects of a fresh lease of earthly life. In the case of Samson, there is what may be called the primrose path of dalliance, of reconciliation with the Philistines—offered as a sensible and feasible proposition by both Manoa and Dalila; certainly, there is the tempting prospect of a cozy, if deceptive, domestic life with Dalila. For the archbishop, there is the alternative of a refuge, if a dubious one, in France. Both the protagonists reject with contumely the safer course which seems to beckon to them.

In each case the soul is clawed and racked; it is strained to the highest pitch of self-questioning. At this elevation the protagonist functions far above the comprehension of those physically around. He is a centre of consciouseness, operant, now fitfully, now steadily, which increasingly asserts and presses itself against both uncomprehending friendly forces and an avowedly hostile phalanx of opposition. The light of faith burns more steadily in the heart of Thomas. But that is easily explained.

The occasional vacillations and backsliding on the part of Samson are sufficiently explained by the enormity of sufferings he has undergone. In fact, these backslidings help to make the character credible, for the reader or spectator recognises that here is a human being and no divine monstrosity. From this recognition stems sympathy. Besides, whenever he gives way to despair, he does not take long to recover his faith. An overwhelming sense of personal suffering may temporarily eclipse his faith, but before long it reasserts itself and resumes its intense glow. The sense of a divine superintendence and guardianship articulates itself now and again in the depths of his soul, and finally spills over into his stately utterances.

The juxtaposition of two levels of consciousness—one in varying degrees of relationship or contact with the divine will or purpose and the other rather earth-creeping even when claiming full comprehension or knowledge—makes for a striking dramatic effect. The simultaneous operation of these two levels of consciousness produces a dual movement through most of each work much like an antiphonal chant: the voice of nescience and the voice of knowledge.

Samson's manner of acting at the decisive moment baffles the chorus, almost leaves it witless, nearly in the same way as the archbishop's making an irrevocable choice disconcerts, almost stuns, the attending priests. To the priest's exhortation:

> You would bar the door
> Against the lion, the leopard, the wolf or boar,
> Why not more
> Against beasts with the souls of damned men, against men
> Who would damn themselves to beasts.

Thomas replies:

> You think me reckless, desparate and mad.
> You argue by results, as this world does,
> To settle if an act be good or bad
> You defer to the fact....
> It is out of time that may decision is taken
> If you call that decision
> To which my whole being gives entire consent.

And in the other play the chorus's puzzled ejaculation 'How thou wilt here come off surmounts my reach' is thus answered by Samson:

> Be of good courage; I begin to feel
> Some rousing motions in me, which dispose
> To something extraordinary my thoughts.

The brief comparative study made above, which is in the nature of an interlude, is designed to pinpoint a certain significant similarity in the thrust of the dramatic argument as it reveals itself in either play. For both the protagonists man and God are exclusive terms of a proposition that demands acceptance of the one and rejection of the other. As Thomas says: 'I give my life/To the Law of God above the Law of Man.' The vision of a spiritual fulfilment is dramatised in either work through the nature of the protagonist's response to the competing claims of man and God, of the temporal and eternal.

Now to look at *Samson Agonistes* alone. The vision embodied there is born of a travail-an agonised trial having for is essential components a certain complex of abominations which are the means of at once harrowing and purging the hero's soul.

Samson's present existential ccondition, his father's proposed 'solicitations' to the Philistine lords, his remembrance and the subsequent appearance of Delilah, that 'deceitful concubine', the hollow vaunting of Harapha, that 'baffled coward'-are all singularly abominable, while what is even more so is the enormity of his own folly, or 'sin' as Samson views it. But is so comes about that Samson has perforce to endure these abominations if only to get over them even as a pilgrim has to get over such hurdles as may be put on his way to test the fibres of his moral and spiritual being.

The anguish bred by the enormity of his own folly is infinitely augmented by having to bear and absorb the shock resulting from the pitiless onslaughts made by Dalila and Harapha, and not very slightly by Manoa himself.

The moral ugliness represented in Dalila and Harapha appears loathsome and revolting in the extreme and is made the more execrable when contrasted with the unrelenting refusal of Samson to do business with any form or shape of evil. This refusal has everything religious, rather puritanic about it, and it is enacted with the plenary force of his entire being. This refusal is a peremptory gesture of his revived self operating in an aura of Beauty and Truth as he glimpses them. One recalls the famous observation of Keats, 'The excellence of every art is its intensity, capable of making all disagreeables evaporate from their close relationship with Beauty and Truth.' (Letter of December 21, 1817). Thus viewed, the intensity of *Samson Agonistes* makes the abominations, to which we have referred, evaporate from their close relationship with Samson's fresh-lit, severe vision of what is true and beautiful and the unpleasantness of Samson's encounters with Dalila, Harapha, the Philistine officer and Manoa is sunk in the 'momentous depth of speculation' excited by them.

Samson can make himself acceptable to his God by self-conquest and this self-conquest is achievable through identifying and then completely repudiating and excluding from his being those all too instictive urges which are both peculiarly of this world and of a kind that precludes all spiritual growth.

The Manoa, Dalila and Harapha episodes can thus be regarded as Milton's dramatic objectifications of those instinctive urges which serve to keep man in bondage to this world. These may, in a sense, be considered as 'objective correlative' to use Eliot's phrase. And not only Manoa,Dalila and Harapha;even the chorus can be treated as an objective correlative. Manoa represents the solicitous paternal endeavours of which one in the position of the haplesss Samson would be only too tempted to take advantage. Delilah, under the initial garb of penitence, offers the prospect, however questionable, of a fresh lease of conjugal life-a prospect which would not be very easy to resist. Harapha represents a bully's invitation to submit, and again such an invitation cannot but tempt one as sorely handicapped as Samson is at the moment. The chorus, which as a friendly force, can be looked upon as an extension of Samson with reference to his past, present and future, performs a number of functions. It at once eulogises Samsons's heroic past, lapses into despairing interrogation of God's will and rises, in the midst of occasional bafflements, into a confident prophecy of Samson's redemption.

An urge to take an easy refuge with a Manona or even a Dalila, however treacherous, especially when they offer to take him back, has an unquestionable credibility in view of the crippling circumstances of Samson. So also is an urge to capitulate, however heroic the past. The rather ambivalent posture of the chorus is basically that of Samson himself.

From the dramatic point of view, these urges and propensities whose shadows at least are likely to be there in the mind and heart of the long-harassed protagonist, need to be identified and brought to the fore. The protagonist needs to be made to meet these situations publicly and repudiate the temptations involved. Therefore, these dramatic situations may as well be looked upon as powerfully suggestive extensions or better, externalisations, of certain latent facets of Samson's own consciousness. The profane tendencies are brought out in the open only to be cast aside.

The spirit of exclusion which distinguishes, as we have seen, the vision of recovery and triumph even extends to the dramatic technique. And this rather negative spirit of rejection is inevitably and invariably accompanied by a corresponding positive spirit of emphasis. Thus when we come round to look at, and discuss, the dramatic technique, we see a grim rejection going hand in hand with a grinding emphasis.

In fact, *Samson Agonistes* is a marvel of exclusive emphasis. The intensity of concentration, which is the result of this emphasis, is achieved at the expense of whatever might conceivably distract attention from the momentous issue of Samson's predicament and its final resolution. Throughout the play the focus is such as to simultaneously secure illumination of the theme and obliteration of all else.

Caroline Spurgeon has spoken of 'recurrent images' playing 'a part in raising, developing, sustaining, and repeating emotion' in Shakespeare's tragedies. In *Samson Agonistes* we notice what we may call a recurrence of the mind's fastening or obsessive dwelling on a fact, an idea, a raging passion. A remarkable feature of the dramatic mechanism of *Samson Agonistes* is an unremitting iteration of ideas and facts-the iteration being carried on in each single case in a slightly varying language.

A brief analysis of Samson's opening speech will show how the device of iteration is at work. Here Milton underscores the hero's dismal plight-the objective reality as also the turmoil of the inner world. And how does he go about it?

His being a blind captive in the Philistine prisonhouse, subjected to ignominous toil, constitutes the objective reality for Samson. The inner world, the mind, is a battleground, a maelstrom of sizzling currents of thought-each pulling him in its own direction, so that he is sorely tried-he is bruised, battered and he bleeds. He reflects on the apparent irony of the heavenly prophecy before his birth, in the context of his present degradation. He broods on the ironical use of his superhuman strength in the service of his enemy. He bewails his loss of eyesight. At the same time, however he cautions himself against calling in question the will of Providence, since he is conscious of his own transgression in having let out the secret entrusted to him at the importunity of a woman.

Our present exercise is aimed at showing how each of these elements is harped on, in conjuction with the rest by the repetitive method. The abomination of his servitude is conveyed thus: 'my task of servile toil,/-Daily in the common prison else enjoined me,/Where I, a prisoner chained'; 'Made of my enemies the scorn and gaze,/To grind in brazen fetters'; 'Put to the labour of a beast, debased/Lower than bond-slave! 'Himself in bonds under Philistian yoke/Life in captivity/Among inhuman foes'.

Mark the manner of driving home the loss of sight: 'if I must die/-Betrayed, captived, and both my eyes put out': 'and find him/eyeless in Gaza'; But, chief af all,/ O loss of Sight, of thee I most Complaint Blind among, enemies!; 'light, the Prime work of God to me is/ extinct' 'I, dark in light, exposed/ To daily fraud, contempt, abuse, and wrong'; 'O dark, dark, dark, amid the blaze of noon,/Irrecoverably dark, total eclipse/Without all hope of day!'

The irony involved in the contrast between his promised greatness and his present wretchedness is emphasized in Samson's repeated questioning of the ways of God: 'Oh, wherefore was my birth from Heaven foretold/Twice by an Angel....?' or 'Why was my breeding ordered and prescribed/As of a person separate to God if I must die/Betrayed, captived' or 'Promise was that I/should Israel from Philistian yoke deliver!/Ask for this great deliverer now.' His sense of shame and anguish at the thought of his strength being prostituted in the service of the Philistine, whom he should already have destroyed, is conveyed through reiteration. What a shame to 'grind in brazen fetters under task/With this heaven-gifted strenght!' or 'O glorious strength,/ Put to the labour of a beast.....'

Similar is the method of expressing his sense of transgression and his spirit of self-questioning, self-reproach and humility:

> Yet stay; let me not rashly call in doubt
> Divine prediction. What if all foretold
> Had been fulfilled but through my own default?
> Whom have I to complain of but myself....?

Again

> But peace! I must not quarrel with the will
> Of highest dispensation, which herein
> Haply hath ends above my reach to know

All this is from Samson's opening speech. It needs pointing out that the thoughts dwelt upon above have been pursued with even greater obstinacy in the rest of the work.

The first four tiny words of the Chorus involving a repetition of 'this'- This, this is he'- would seem to pull off a sharpening of the focus on the hero to such a point of intensity as to put all else out of existence, as it were. All meaningful existence is suddenly contracted to the person of Samson. The near-incredulity, expressed through a slightly modified iteration of the first four words ('Can this be he....'), is the means of providing a flash-back to Samson's past which is a saga of heroic feats attended by divine inspiration and support. Barring the recounting of the heroic deeds, which is dramatically designed to drive home the specially regrettable character of his present impotence, references to both the present and the past of the protagonist are part of the iterative procedure we have been talking about.

The next question of the Chorus (Which shall I first bewail-Thy bondage or lost sight,/prison within prison/Inseparably drak?') involves no extension of the universe of discourse, but is designed only to reinforce the impression of the hero's double calamity. And once again the Chorus dwells upon Samson's fall from grace and his having touched the very nadir of his fortune: 'from the top of wonderous glory/To lowest pitch of abject fortune thou art fallen!' We have seen the Chorus already alluding to the same fact of misfortune in different words. Besides, the Chorus's shocked exclamation.

> Can this be he,
> That heroic, that renowned
> Irresistible Samson? Whom, unarmed,
> No strength of man, or fiercest wild beast could withstand?

is echoed in a strikingly similar language by Manoa a little later:

> Is this the man
> That invincible Samson, far renowed,
> The dread of Israel's foes......
> Who single combatant
> Duelled their armies.....
> Himself an army.....

The sad divorce between strength and wisdom which accounted for Samson giving away the divinely entrusted secret to Dalila, and thus to his enemies, is, whether directly or otherwise, again a recurrent theme. Strength without wisdom is a burden, a mockery. Like a refrain, it runs through a good part of the play. Samson wails;

> O impotence of mind in body strong
> But what is strength without a double share
> Of wisdom? Vast, unwieldy, burdensome,
> Proudly secure, yet liable to fall
> By weakest subtleties; not made to rule,
> But to subserve where wisdom bears command....

Says the Chorus:

> But thee, whose strength, while virtue was her mate
> Might have subdued the Earth....

And again Samson:

Immeasurable strength they might behold
In me; of wisdom nothing more than mean.
This with the other should atleast have paired;
These two, proportioned ill, drove me transverse.

How obsessively Samson chastises himself for surrendering his secret to Dalila can be seen from the almost unceasing iteration marking his looking back at that incident. He cannot forgive himself for his profane act leading to his disastrous fall. He is harder on himself than on Delilah. Thus to the Chorus:

Of what I now suffer
She was not the prime cause, but I myself,
Who, vanquished with a peal of words (O weakness!)
Gave up my fort of silence to a woman.

And again to the Chorus:

..... had I sight, confused with shame
How could I once look up, or heave the head
Who, like a foolish pilot, have shipwrecked
My vessel trusted to me from above,
Gloriously rigged, and for a word, a tear
Fool! have divulged the secret gift of God
To a deceitful woman.

To Manoa:

If aught seem vile
As vile hath been my folly, who have profaned
The mystery of God, given me under pledge
Of vow, and have betrayed it to a woman....

and

But I God's counsel have not kept, His holy secret
Presumptuously have published, impiously,
Weakly at least and shamefully-a sin...

and

Then, swollen with pride, into the snare I fell
Of fair fallacious looks, venereal trains,

Softened with pleasure and voluptuous life,
At length to lay my head and hallowed pledge
Of all my strength in the lascivious lap
Of a deceitful concubine..

And to Dalila:

I gave, thou say'st, the example.
I led the way-bitter reproach, but true;
I to myself was false ere thou to me.

It is throught iterated emphasis that Samsŏn expresses his iron faith in the superiority of his God to Dagon:

Than thou shalt see, or rather to thy sorrow
Soon feel, whose God is strongest, thine or mine...

which is re-declared in the lines:

...I once again
Defy thee to the trial of mortal fight,
By combat to decide whose God is God,
Thine or whome I with Israel's sons adore.

After having agreed to proceed to Dagon's temple, Samson with sledge-hammering emphasis assures the Chorus that he will conduct himself as a true Nazarite and not dishonour himself or his religion in any way: 'Nothing to do, be sure, that may dishonour/Our Law, or stain my vow of Nazarite'; 'Yet this be sure, in nothing to comply/scandalous or forbidden in our Law? 'Happen what may, of me expect nothing to hear/-Nothing dishonorable, impure, unworthy/ Our Lord, or Law, my nation, or myself'.

The illustrations are suggestive rather than exhaustive. It would appear that by an unsparing manipulation of this re-iterative device, the dramatist achieves his object of securing as much deepening as possible of the tragic experience. And we would suggest that the remarkably intense and concentrative character of this experience has been achieved more by this device than by the mere observance of the 'Unities' and the restriction of the *dramatis personae* to the barest minimum. Not only is the play's great issue kept in an unfailingly steady perspective; the device is also calculated to secure for it that never-to-be mistaken heavy, dense, yet dynamic and ebullient atmosphere, that rather overwhelming impression of pith and substance which marks out *Samson Agonistes* in spite of its all too narrow physical canvas.

Renaissance drama has the attributes of an extrovert as opposed to a play like *Samson Agonistes* which is introvertive. Renaissance drama is expansive with a generous bulk and with audible echoes of happenings in the world around. It is an affirmation of life and the playwright thinks it fit to add to the main plot sub-plots, to the main characters a whole host of subsidiary characters, to the main situation allied situations, so that the work is a miniature world with any number of parallel (and antithetical) characters and situations. The world of a Renaissance tragedy is a remarkably extended world, the intensity of its experience not withstanding. As argued by G.K. Hunter: 'The tendency to pile up examples, to enrich by amassing materials from a wide variety of sources, to treasure the curious detail-these are, from a formal point of view, signs of the Gothic rather than the classic... the idea that tragedy as a classical structure would be "spoiled" by repetition, by addition of side-chapels, secondary plots, new episodes... would not, I suspect, have made a great deal of sense in the period; for the equation of "classicism" with 'purity" had not yet been made. The Gothic mind of the Elizabethan audience exercised a natural sovereignty over the classical past.[5]

Such was the compulsive character of their varied tasted and urges and their nearly omnivorous appetite for experience and ideas that the renaissance has aptly been termed an age of 'syncretism and electicism'.

Far from opening out, Milton's play contracts and narrows. It is far more vertical than horizontal. It is far more exclusive than inclusive. It is based on the denial of life-life as it is commonly understood (*contemptus mundi*) rather than the affirmation of it. It presents a little point of space with just a handful of characters acting and interacting, with the rest of the world shut out. It has no use for, and, in fact, it frowns upon 'the curious detail', 'sidechapels', 'secondary plots' and 'new episodes'. The vision emerging from an inflexible attitude of world-negation dictates the play's form and mechanism. Both the vision and the mechanism bear the unmistakable stamp of Milton's Puritan temper, though the form is clearly Greek. It is no longer a dark, mysterious and fear-ridden world where something called Fate operates. It a is world from which the haunting sense of fear has been dispelled by the assuring light of a new dispensation. Here is a clarity of khowledge regarding God man relationship. Here is the idea of a clearly-understood covenant between man and God. In this Hebraic-Puritan world the sense of guilt results from a conscious breach of that convenant or of a sacred trust under it and has no enigma or riddle attached to it as is the case in Greek drama. This is true of both *Samson Agonistes* and *Paradise Lost*. Hence the severity of temper, of self-flagellation and hence the severely exclusive dramatic technique in *Samson Agonistes* making a highly charged thought turn back, instead of looking sideways for kindred thoughts, upon itself with an air of fatality.

REFERENCES

1. G. Steiner, *The Death of Tragedy* (Faber Books, 1961), p. 32.
2. William P. Parker, *Milton's Debt to Greek Tragedy*, pp. 249-50.
3. F.E. Hutchinson, *Milton and the English Mind*, (1960), p.144.
4. T.S. Eliot, *On Poetry and Poets*, p. 15.
5. G.K. Hunter, 'Seneca and the Elizabethans: A case-study in "Influence",' *Shakespeare Survey: 20*.

SAMSON AGONISTES AND GREEK TRAGEDY

If Eliot's monologues like "The Love Song of J. Alfred Prufrock" or "Gerontion" look back to the techniques of Browning's monologues without reflecting their spirit, so does Milton's *Samson Agonistes* follow the structure of Greek tragedy while working in it a temper which is certainly not Greek. While Milton's peotic genius drew imponderably upon his classical as well as Biblical scholarship the essential temper of his mind always remained Judaic-Christian. He let his profound classical knowledge come as grist to his Judeo-Christian mill.

In his introducton to *Samson Agonistes* Milton dwells upon the classical conception of tragedy with veneration. He writes:

"Tragedy, as it was anciently composed, hath been ever held the gravest, moralest, and more profitable of all other poems; therefore said by Aristotle to be of power, by raising pity and fear, or terror, to purge the mind of those and such-like passions-that is, to temper and reduce them to just measure with a kind of delight, stirred up by reading or seeing those passions well imitated.......................

"In the modelling therefore of this poem, with good reason, the Ancients and Italians are rather followed, as of much more authority and fame".

It is not altogether surprising, therefore, that the following comment is rather typical of the generality of critical attitude towards *Samson Agonistes.*

"Milton was deeply influenced by the content as well as the form of ancient tragedy".[1]

A.S.P. Woodhouse hits the nail on the head when he observes: "Misled by Milton's prefatory emphasis on his Greek models, an emphasis entirely justified if properly understood, critics have assumed that the poet intended not only to follow them in structure and convention but to reproduce their spirit and effect, and that hence the only criterion for judging *Samson Agonistes* is Greek Tragedy".[2]

I propose in this essay to try to get at the essential temper of Samson's mind as revealed in *Samson Agonistes* by examining it in close relation to the mental cast of the protagonists of some representative Greek tragedies.

It will be seen that neither Oedipus, nor Prometheus, nor Philoctetes (the Greek tragic heroes Samson is usually compared with) shares the peculiar temper of Samson's mind in its absolute clarity of knowledge not only regarding the relationship between the human and the divine but, more particularly, regarding his present tragic impasse and the cause thereof.

Over the Greek world hangs the ironic shadow of what one may call Fate, Destiny or Necessity, and the actors on the stage of human life are of tener than not brought down without their being conscious of any sense of guilt. Without having knowingly perpetrated any wrong, without having consciously violated any code, pledge, or any sacred agreement to which their whole being gave assent, these personages feel tripped up in the dark and caught in a blinding mist, and are racked with pain. The impression is inescapable that a person need not be directly responsible for what is happening to him, and Gloucester's observation, albeit in a different context, ('As flies to wanton boys are we to the gods,/They kill us for their sport') does serve the purpose of a plausible commentary on the Greek situation with whatever reservations there may be.

For it is indeed a mighty, fearsome spider's web-the order of necessity determining this sublunary human life and there is hardly any knowing when an unwary mortal will be badly caught in it. The awe-some shadow often operates in the form of a curse upon one royal house or another. Sometimes the sufferings of an individual (for example, Hippolytus) are the result of a god or goddess being affronted, and the gods and goddesses are scarcely less touchy than the men and women who are supposed to adore them. If the quarrel between Artemis and Aphrodite results in the tragedy of Hippolytus, the fates of the contenders at the Trojan War were largely determined by the feuds and jealousies of the rival goods and goddesses. Moving and compulsively gripping as the tales are, the impression remains that the human actors are being tortured and sacrificed on a mighty chess-board devised to suit the sadistic humours of the olympians. And a full knowledge of the cause-effect relationship woven by the dark hand of fate is often denied to the humans who, consequently, are not capable of relating thier sufferings to their conscious will. Or, even when such knowledge does exist, what is singularly missing is any owning up or recognition of conscious folly. Thus Oedipus speaks to Jocasta as it begains to dawn upon him that he has been caught unawares in the coils of fate:

> O God, I think I have called curses on myself in Ignorance,..... Would not one rightly judge and say that on me, These things were sent by some malignant God?[3]

When the brazen-faced Creon accuses the blind Oedipus in Athens of parricide and incest, the latter advances the following defence:

The bloody deaths, the incest, the calamities
You speak so glibly of I suffered them,
By fate, against my will! It was God's pleasure
And perhaps our race had angered him long ago.
In me myself you could not find such evil
As would have made me sin against my own.
And tell me this: if there were prophecies
Repeated by the oracles of the gods,
That father's death should come throught his own son,
How could you justly blame it upon me?
On me, who was yet unborn, yet unconceived,
Not yet existent for my father and mother?
If then I came into the world-as I did come-
In wretchedness, and met my father in fight,
And knocked him down, not knowing that I killed him
Now whom I killed-again, how could you find
Guilt in that unmediated act?
As for my mother-damn you you have no shame,
Thought you are her own brother, in forcing me
To speak of that unspeakable marriage;
But I shall speak, I'll not be silent now
After you've let your foul talk go so far!
Yes, she gave me birth-incredible fate!
But neither of us knew the truth; and she
Bore my children also-and then her shame.
But one thing I do know: you are content
To slander her as well as me for that;
While I would not have married her willingly
Nor willingly would I ever speak of it
No: I shall not be judged an evil man,
Neither in that marriage nor in that death
Which you forever charge me with so bitterly.[4]

Prometheus is persuaded that he is being held in chains and tortured by tyrant, and ungodly God, who had received services from him before only to prove treacherous later.

These were the services

I rendered to this tyrant and these pains
The payment he has given me in requital-
This is a sickness rooted and inherent in the nature of a tyranny:
That he that holds it does not trust his friends...............
Pitiless is he that thus chastises me, a spectacle
Bringing dishonour on the name of Zeus.[5]

The images of oppressor and oppressed remain till the end of the play:

O Holy mother mine,
O sky that circling brings the light to all,
You see me, how I suffer, how unjustly.

And now listen to Philoctetes who has been "alone and very wretched, without friend or comrade, suffering a great deal". He is speaking to Neoptolemus;

.... nothing evil has yet perished,
The gods somehow give them most excellent care
They find their pleasure in turning back from death
The rogues and tricksters, but the just and good
They are always sending out cf the world.
How can I reckon the score, how can I praise
When praising Heaven I find the gods are bad?[7]

How, then, do the suffering heroes view and seek to explain their tragedy? Philoctetes is convinced of being entirely blameless and of the gods being unaccountably hostile. Prometheus is not only unaware of having done any wrong but also unwaveringly convinced of having done some conspicuous service, in the first instance, to Zeus and then to man, the latter act serving to make Zeus implacably hostile. Oedipus while recognising his being involved in horrible sins, repudiates, in the clearest terms, the charge of conscious responsibility for parricide and incest. He not only proclaims but believes,as we do, that he is a hapless victim rather than a conscious agent.

Hippolytus, when brought to his sad pass, is seen to guess at the cause of his tragedy:

This evil comes from some manslaying of old,
Some ancient tale of murder among my kin.[8]

Oedipus has the same turn of mind and speaks in the same vein:

It was God's pleasure,
And perhaps our race had angered him long ago.[9]

One is aware that there is a profound moral vision to be deciphered in each of these great tragedies and that one would always remain tagged on tò the surface of the things unless an adequate attempt were made to comprehend the visions enacted in these tales in the light of the Greek conception of 'Dike' and the peculiar suspectibility of the personages concerned, ironically aiding in the fulfilment of the supernatural designs. What we mean is that the movement of the hero's mind and will is such as to be frightfully in consonance with the gods' designs. Each of the heroes can be seen to be guilty of *hubris* in one shape or another and to act in a way such as simultaneously to work his ruin and carry out the divine will.

We may be seen to have laboured the point at too great a length. But then our purpose is to bring the difference in the attitudes of these heroes and that of milton's hero into the clearest and sharpest possible focus. If,as we have seen, the Greek tragic characters blame either the gods or some misdoings of their forbears for the fate that has overtaken them, Samson blames his misfortune entirely on himself. Let us listen to Samson:

> Yet stay; let me not rashly call in doubt
> Divine prediction. What if all fortold
> Had been fulfilled but throught my own default?
> Whom have I to complain of but myself,
> Who this high gift of strength committed to me,
> In what part lodged, how easily bereft me,
> Under the seal of silence could not keep
> But weakly to a woman must reveal it,
> O'ercome with importunity and tears?
> O impotence of mind in body strong!

He calls himself a 'foolish pilot' who has 'shipwrecked my veseel trusted to me from above'.

He asks:

> Tell me, friends,
> Am I not sung and proverbed for a fool
> In every street? Do they not say 'How well
> Are come upon him his deserts?

Then,

> Of what I now suffer
> She (Dalila) was not the prime cause, but I myself,
> Who, vanquished with a peal of words, (O weakness!)
> Gave up my fort of silence to a woman.

When Manoa calls in question the justice of God's ways to Samson, the latter replies:-

Appoint not heavenly disposition, father.
Nothing of all these evils hath befallen me
But justly, myself have brought them on;
Sole author I, sole causes.
....
I yielded, and unlocked all my heart
Who, with a grain of manhood well resolved,
Might easily have shook off all her snares.
But foul effiminacy held me yoked
Her bond-slave. O indignity, O blot
To honour and religion! Servile mind
Rewarded well with servile punishment!

And in like accents he goes on with a kind of stubborn fury. His arraigning himself is a frightening process of self-abasement which involves a clear-eyed recognition of his unspeakable folly and an unambiguous acknowledgement of the justice of God's ways, of the treatment God has meted out to him. As we have seen, Manoa would have God deal with his once-valued champion in a different way. So does the chorus more than once. Even Samson on occasion yields to this temptation. But the one impression that remains steady and clear is that, of his own admission, he has sinned and his sufferings are well-merited. We cannot imagine Samson saying as a Greek character does:

A God tripped up my judgement.

As Grierson says:

"When the play opens we see him (Samson) repentant, admitting to the full that the fault is his own. Whatever the chorus may say or sing of the mysteries of God's dealings with man, as is the manner of Choruses in Greek Drama, Samson is quite clear on the fact that he is where is because of his own contemptible weakness in yielding to his wife".[10]

This brings us to another important aspect of our consideration of this play.

If Greek drama is religious, as it obviously is from a certain point of view, then, *Samson Agonistes* is no less so. A religious drama cannot be properly understood except in the context of the divine background against which the action at the human level takes place.The divine scheme of things, the divine order and the divine purpose are an essential part of a religious play's field of reference. In fact, the basic theme of a religious play cannot but be some variation or other of God-man relationship, of the ways of God to man. God is involved, in the affairs of man, His will operates in them and the final outcome is controlled by it, whether directly of indirectly. The Greek plays talk of the ways of Zeus, of Aphrodite, of Athene and Poseidon, among others. Milton's play talks of the ways of the one God he and his hero believe in, to man. On this interpenetration of the divine and the human, Kitto observes:

'Religious drama contains gods as well as men, and where gods are present they must take precedence. Only when the human drama in the foreground is seen against the background of divine action is the structure and significance of the play truly seen!'[11]

Now, according to Kitto, there is all the difference between religious drama and the kind of tragedy that the Aristotelian rules suggest. The latter he would call tragedy of character. The difference is explained by the fact while in the former the principal focus is upon the world-order, whether already stable or in a state of evolution which could just snuff out or crush indiviuals, however great or mighty they may appear to us, in a tragedy of character attention is focussed upon the hero, on why and how he acts, without any attempt being made to create an awareness of an all-embracing world-order. Thus the drama that Aristotle has in mind or which his theory would point to can be called humanistic or secular.

Kitto makes it clear that 'Religious drama is not peculiarly Greek though the Greeks had their own ways of presenting it'. 'We are given the feeling that the Universe is coherent, even though we may not understand it completely'. Discussing the tragedy of Oedipus, he observes: '.. although life has been so cruel to Oedipus, nevertheless it is not a chaos'

"When Aeschylus depicts a conflict between one god and another, which clearly is a sign of a disordered universe, the reason is plain enough: he is depicting a world-order in the process of evolution. In the end, Zeus reigns without opposition. When Sophocles represents Oedipus as being destroyed though essentially innocent, he is not presuming a flaw in the universe but recongnising that its majestic order may cut the thread of a single life and requite venal unwisdom with utterly disproportionate penalties, just as he recognises that when the insensibility of a Creon disturbs the path of Dike, then an Antigone or a Haemon and an Eurydice may be destroyed. In these plays the innocent do suffer, and their suffering is not 'revolting'; and the reason for this is that their suffering is seen to be part of a world-order, which though not always beneficent, is at least intelligible".[12]

Let us now look at *Samson Agonistes*. It conforms to Greek tragedy in its obvious suggestion of a divine background to whatever is happening before us. Like Greek tragedy, it involves the assumption of a world-order in which divine superintendence and control presents itself as an unmistakable feature. In fact, the figure of Samson is unintelligible except in terms of a mystic thread binding him to his God, of his having been chosen by him, of his having grown up and thrived "under His special eye" and of his being 'led on to mightiest deeds'. Paradoxically, however, this very feature would seem, as we shall see soon, to set *Samson Agonistes* apart from the tragedy of antiquity. Indeed, in point of substance, Samson is neither Aristotelian not like the Greek drama of Kitto's description beyond a certain point.

Samson is not truly Aristotelian in so far as it does not pass from happiness to misery (Samson is not happy when the play opens) and because there is no *hamartia* in evidence within the ambit of the play. Without going beyond the bounds of the play one could only see Samson passing from misery to happiness, for when we first meet him, Samson is characterised by a loss of the power which is divine grace and his end is marked by a form of suicide which represents a return to grace. As for *hamartia,* there is none during the entire action of the play; the error of judgement causing his lapsed state and blindness and misery is a thing of the past as far as the play is concerned. Structurally, Samson is Aristotelian in so far as it embodies *peripetia, anagnorisis* and *denonuement* and in its use of the chorus, the messenger and the speech-device called stichomythia.

It is substantially unlike greek drama, for, the innocent do not suffer here, nor does the moral order operate like the wheels of juggernaut, heedless of the human cry for happiness. The world-order embodied in *Samson* is not only intelligible but also beneficent. And its intelligibility and beneficence are not only perceived by the reader or spectator but by the protagonist himself.

In another respect, too, Samson is at a far remove from any of the characters in Greek drama. Samson is the elect of God to accomplish a mission. His conception and birth were divinely heralded and so was his appointed task. To be chosen by God, to be reared under his guidance for the accomplishment of a sacred task is a peculiarly Biblical conception without a parallel in Greek thought. It speaks of a special sort of relationship between God and humanity, a personal relationship signifying his loving solicitude for his creation, his superintendence and a watchful and benign providence. For those who are chosen and therefore fore-ordained to high glory and bliss are the souls through whom the divine will in relation to humanity is carried out. The Bible speaks of 'them who are called according to his purpose. For whom he did foreknow, he also did predestinate to be conformed to the image of his Son, that he might be the first born among many brethren. Moreover, whom he did predestinate, them he also called: and whom he called, them he also justified: and whom he justified, them he also glorified".[13]

In *Paradise Lost* the Almighty tells the Son while forevisioning the success of Satan in making man transgress:

> Some I have chosen of peculiar grace
> Elect above the rest, so is My will[14]

A little earlier he had said:

> Man shall not quite be lost, but saved who will
> Yet not of will in him, but grace in Me
> Freely vouchasfed. Once more I will renew
> His lapsed powers though forfiet, and enthralled
> By sin to fatal exorbitant desires:
> Upheld by Me, yet once more he shall stand
> On even ground against his mortal foe
> By me upheld........[15]

Which would seem to suggest that Adam has qualified to be God's elect, for to let him finally be lost would mean letting Satan fulfil his malice and bring to naught God's goodness. This is how argues the Son who refers to Adam as 'Thy creature late so loved, Thy youngest Son'.

It is not hard to see how Samson, God's elect, looks back to Adam, the first human elect, how he resembles Adam in proving false to God, in turning out unworthy of the high privilege and glory God had endowed him with, in how God renews

> His lapsed powers, though forfeit and enthralled
> By sin to foul exorbitant desires..........

and in how he is 'upheld' by the Almighty, so that he can stand once more, on even ground, against his mortal foe. Poetically, this concept of election can be traced lack to God electing his Son to take command of the battle against the rebel angels with a view to their final expulsion from Heaven.

> 'Two days are, therefore, passed; the third is thine:
> For thee I have ordained it, and thus far
> Have suffered, that the glory may be thine
> Of ending this war, since none but thou
> Can end it, Into thee such virtue and grace
> Immense I have transfused, that all may know
> In Heaven and Hell Thy power above compare,
> And this perverse commotion governed thus

To manifest thee worthiest to be Heir
of all things-to be Heir, to be King
By sacred function, they deserved right.
Go, then,thou Mightiest in Thy Father's might;
Ascend my chariot; guide the rapid wheels
That shake Heavens's basis; bring forth all my war;
My bow and thunder, My almighty arms.
Pursue these sons of Darkness, drive them out
From all heaven's bounds into the utter deep;
There let them learn, as likes them, to despise
God,and Messiah His annointed King'.[16]

One would venture to suggest that Samson being chosen to free Israel from the Philistine yoke constitutes a microcosmic reenactment of the Heavenly event alluded to in the above quotation. Both at the supernatural and human levels, God is making his will and purpose known unequivocally by choosing his champions who are raised in their respective spheres to supreme heights of power, rank and glory. Indeed, as the biblical affirmation goes, "whoever is elected is justified and fore-ordained to glory".

The chorus, Manoa and Samson himself give accounts of the incredible feats of valour he had accomplished on behalf of his nation and people under divine inspiration and guidance. God had implanted in him 'immense virtue and grace' that all might know his power 'above compare', being honoured and glorified by the Maker Himself.

Here is how the Chorus recounts Samson's superhuman deeds as God's elect:

Can this be he,
That heroic, that renowned,
Irresistible Samson ? Whom unarmed,
No strength of man, or fiercest wild beast could withstand;
Who tore the lion as the lion tears the kid,
Ran on embattled armies clad in iron,
And weaponless himself,
Made arms ridiculous, useless the forgery
Of brazen shield and spear the hammered cuirass,
Chalbyean-tempered steel, and frock of mail
Adamantean proof:
But safest he who stood aloof,
When insupportably his foot advanced,
In scorn of their proud arms and warlike tools
Spurned them to death by troops. The bold Ascalonite
Fled from his lion camp; old warriors turned

Their plaited backs under his heel
Or grovelling soiled their crested helmet in the dust,
Then with what trival weapon came to hand,
The jaw of a dead ass, his sword of bone,
A thousand foreskins fell, the flower of Palestine,
In Ramath-lechi, famous to this day:
Then by main force pulled up, and on his shoulders bore,
The gates of Azza, post and massy bar,
Up to the hill by Herbon, seat of giants old
Like whom the gentiles feign to bear up Heaven.

When the chorus complains that even though Samson has never been remiss, Israel is still in bondage, Samson blames it all on the perfidies of his tribe whose leading people never acknowledged his divinely appointed mission:

That fault I take not on me, but transfer
On Isreals governors and heads of tribes,
Who seeing those great acts which God had done
Singly by me against his conquerors,
Acknowledged not nor at all considered
Deliverence offered. I, on the other side,
Used no ambition to commend my deeds:
The deeds themselves, though mute spoke loud the doer.

When he 'willingly on some condition' surrendered himself to the men of Judah, they 'as gladly yield me

To the uncircumcised a welcome prey,
Bound with two cords'.

And then?

But cords to me were threads
Touched with the flame: on their whole host I flew
Unarmed, and with a trivial weapon felled
Their choiest youth:

And now Manoa seeing his sons's 'miserable change' is put in mind of his God-inspired heroic past.

Is this the man,
That invincible Samson, a renowned,
The dread of Israel's foes, who with a strength
Equivalent to Angels' walked their streets,
None offering fight; who single combatant,
Duelled their armies ranked in proud array,
Himself an army-

Samson, scattering the enemy host before him and like a flaming apparition striking terror, is unavoidably reminiscent of the Son's smashing his way into the ranks of rebel angels and putting them to abject retreat and flight. When the Son sets to work against the rebel host, it is God's wrath at work. Almost likewise, through Samson dealing death and destruction to his enemy operates divine anger.

In *Samson Agonistes* is dramatised a recurrent phenomenon in history—the phenomenon of the divine appointee being rejected by his own people (who prefer servitude to freedom) and being finally vindicated. Thus viewed, the play has a double focus-a focus simultaneously on the conscious predicament of the hero and the unconscious, and therefore the more deplorable, predicament of the nation he was meant to serve and glorify.

But what more often in nations grown corrupt,
And by their vices brought to servitude,
Than to love bondage more than liberty-
Bondage with ease than strenuous liberty-
And to despise, or envy, or suspect,
Whom God hath of His special favour raised
As their deliverer? If he aught begin,
How frequent to desert him, and at last,
To heap ingratitude on worthiest deeds!

The chorus lamenting his present pass almost calls in question God's judgement in treating his champion in an uneven manner.

But such as thou hast solemnly elected,
With gifts, graces eminently adorned,
To some great work, Thy glory,
And people's safety, which in part they effect.
Yet toward these, thus dignified, thou oft,
Amidst their highth of noon
Changest Thy countenance and Thy hand, with no regard
Of highest favours past
From thee on them or them to thee of service.......
....
So deal not with this once Thy glorious champion
The image of thy strength, and mighty minister;

Perhaps the most powerfully operating elements in Samson's consciousness is a razor-keen awareness of his divine pedigree, of his derivation from God. This is nowhere more manifest than during his encounter with Harapha. The study in contrast between the two champions has been tellingly dramatised. Look at how the chorus describes Harapha:

I know him by his stride,

The giant Harapha of Gath, his look,
Haughty, as is his pile high-built and proud.

It is already the picture of a 'haughty' and 'proud' giant, hollow of content. It is the picture of a spiritual fraud. This picture of a spiritual havenot is borne out by the entire dialogue. In the face of Samson's challenge he panics, declines the offered contest on one pretext or another, all reeking with abuse and finally quits crest-fallen. Superstitious and therefore spiritually blind, he is unable to understand the true origin of Samson's strength which he would rather explain in terms of 'spells/And enchantments, some magician's art.' According to him, Samson's claim that he derived all his strength from Heaven at his very birth and that it was 'given thee in thy hair/Where strength can least abide' is a 'feigned', false claim. Stepped in supersitition, he remains impervious to the ways of God, of true religion. He is pitiably alien to the concept of God making his elect the vehicle of his energy and will, transfusing special virtue and grace into a mortal's being. Notwithstanding his pile 'high-built', he remains a wreck, moral and spiritual, with an utter incapacity for understanding true faith.

And now listen to Samson, to his singular fluency of faith and to his animated accents.

I know no spells, use no forbidden arts;
My turst is in the Living God, who gave me,
At my nativity, this strength diffused
No less through all my sinews, joints, and bones,
Than thine, while I preserved these locks unshorn,
The pledge of my unviolated vow.
For proof hereof, if Dagon be thy God,
Go to his temple, invocate his aid.
With solemnest devotion, spread before him
How highly concerns his glory now
To frustrate and dissolve these magic spells
Which I to be the power of Israel's God
Avow, and challenge Dagon to the test
Offering to combat thee, his champion bold,
With the utmost of his godhead seconded:

In reply to Harapha's taunt that Samson has lost all his credentials, that he has been disowned and thrown into the-"common prison' by the very God whose name he so proudly invokes, Samson has the following to say:

All these indignities, for such they are
From thine, these evils I deserve and more,

Acknowledge them from God inflicted on me
Justly, yet despair not his final pardon,
Whose ear is ever open, and His eye
Gracious to re-admit the suppliant;
In confidence whereof I once again
Defy thee to the trial of mortal fight,
By combat to decide whose God is God,
Thine, or whom I with Israel's son Adore.

One hears the clear accents of a true devotee, the currents of whose soul are sustained and nourished by a burning faith-a faith that is never to be quenched. It is the voice of a devout soul full of deep humility and firm confidence.

With no touch of bragging in it, this voice shows the contending one in its true colours. Indeed, the other voice is one of loud vaunting, for it has never known the nourishment of a living faith. It is crude, coarse, obscene.

It must not escape notice that to match Samson's claim, Harapha cannot talk in terms of a comparably strong and intimate relationship with his God. All he is capable of doing is to indulge in vituperation and empty threats. His entire bearing and performance are of a piece with the tone of his self-introduction:

I come not, Samson, to condole they chance
As these perhaps, yet wish it had not been
Though for no friendly intent, I am of Gath,
Men call me Harapha, of stock renowned.............

Critics find Samson proud and even vain. In the course of a comparative study of *Samson Agonistes* and Holderlin's *The Death of Empedocles*, Michael Hamburger says that Holderlin "might have thought Milton's hero just a little bit smug, a little bit priggish even, and more than a little barbaric". He goes on, "Samson's hubris is not sufficiently purged by 'total separation' from his God. Samson's outward pride remains unbroken, as the scene with Dalila shows; and so does his immense egotism-the 'alcohol of egotism' which Coleridge discovered in Milton's Satan'![17] It is so difficult to agree with this view of Samson even when one knows that there is more than one way of looking at a character. If there was any hubris at all in Samson, it took the form of a spirit of self-sufficiency and pride, making him part with his 'mystery' to Dalila and alienating him from God. But that happened before the play began, and after it begins there is no hubris any more., What there is, is but the suffering, consequent upon the act of disobedience. What has been called Samson's pride in the Dalila scene is but pugnacious rebuttal of specious pleas and a dour resistance to what he sees as a renewed approach of the evil that had earlier overcome him and brought on Heaven's desertion. It is more or less the same spirit of resistance that Samson displays in his encounters with Manoa and Harapha. Indeed, it was a much-needed toughening of his spirit acting as a shield against weakening temptations. He can never be too sure about his being on his guard; hence an impression of acerbity. His lashing out at Dalila is easily understandable in the context of his remembering, at the sight of her, the trap she had made him walk into. Indeed, if there is any exhibition of pride in the play as there is, it had better be located in Harapha. It is the stupid pride of a self-enclosed person unable to relate hiself in any significant manner to his tribe, to his God. The immense egotism that Hamburger speaks of can only be ascribed to Harapha. It is not a little amazing to see Samson being equated to Satan. In *Paradise Lost* Satan is disobedient from beginning to end. In *Samson Agonistes* Samson embodies the very spirt of obedience and reproves himself unceasingly for his having been disobedient in a moment of infatuation, with all the terrible consequences that ensued. He resembles Adam who disobeyed likewise with catastrophic consequences. If Adam, soon after the moments of self-indulgence, curses himself and turns deeply contrite asking for divine forgiveness, so does Samson whose self-flagellation would never seem to cease. In fact, as we have already suggested, Samson gives all the indications of being a man of profound humility such as a true servant of God should be.

No doubt, all the three of them-Manoa, Dalila and Harapha-accuse him of pride even though the language of accusation varies.

For Manoa it is a sign of overmuch pride that Samson should be preferring death to release on the procurement of ransom.

> Be penitent, and for thy fault contrite;
> But act not in thy own affliction, son.
> Repent the Sin; but, if the punishment
> Thou cans't avoid, self-preservation bids;
> God will relent, and quit thee of all His debt:
> Who ever more approves and more accepts
> (Best pleased with humble and filial submission)
> Him who imploring mercy, sues for life,

Than who, 'self-rigorous, chooses death as due;
Which argues over-just, and self-displeased
For self-offence more than for God offended.

Manoa's words are often cited to support the charge of pride against Samson. It only needs to be pointed out that Manoa completely misjudges Samson's character, his mental disposition. Which is not surprising since, first, he is a father who would be only too happy to persuade his son to agree to his terms for his return home on the strength of whatever arguments there may be, and, secondly, he cannot be expected to rise to the level of Samson's thoughts, Samson being out and out extraordinary, being God's elect.

Indeed, how can Samson forget that having been raised by God, he owed total commitment to his will? He has proved false and his situation is seemingly without remedy. He is indeed 'self-rigorous', but his being so springs from his consciouses of corruption within himself. He is hard on his apostate self. He is self-displeased. Indeed, he is displeased with his debased self. He is conscious of self-offence because he has offended his inner being. The lower self has got the better of the higher. The road to self-transcendence and recovery of grace lies through self-severity. The sense of his derivation from God entails the need for absolute purity. He is his God's vessel and the vessel must be kept clean and uncontaminated. His most mortifying thought is that he has not been able to keep it so because of laxity, of a lack of self-control in a moment of self-forgetfulness and 'forgetfulness' of his God, of all that he had owed to Him. How can his contrite and expiating self forget that damning lapse? How can he be less than self-rigorous? This is not pride. It is rather an index of his true insight in the situation.

Dalila has failed to make any dent on Samson's mind. The sorely disappointed woman takes leave, saying, among other things,

'To I see thou art implacable, more deaf
To prayers than winds and seas: Yet winds to seas
Are reconciled at length, and sea to shore:
Thy anger unappeasable, still rages,
Eternal tempest never to be calmed.

The humanist answer would be that winds may get reconciled to seas, and 'sea to shore' because these are without a mind. A man in possession of a mind is expected to judge, weigh, to discriminate so that where there is recognition of a damning lapse causing separation from God, there cannot be any soft-pedalling, no playing down; the mind viewing it has to be rigorous and forbidding. In fact, the 'anger unappeasable' is proof that the soul has not atrophied, that if can yet rejoin its source and rejuvenate itself.

As for Harapha's accusation, we have seen what it is worth. He is a casual, arbitrary inorganic thing, and therefore insensately proud. Samson is unflinchingly humble because he is irremovably anchored in his God.

Charles Williams has a beautiful thing to say while differentiating Satan from the Son, the angels, Adam and Eve:

"Precisely as the mark of Satan and the rebel angels is that they will not consent to be derived from any one else; he will have it that he was like Topsy and grew by himself; so the mark of the Son, of the angels, of Adam, of Eve, is that they derive, and take delight in deriving from some one else. Their joy is in that derivation - in love".[18]

As we have tried to show, Samson is all too conscious of being derived and his joy and happiness is in that derivation. When, still refusing to obey the Philistines, Samson asks the chorus -

Shall I abuse this consecrated gift
Of strength, again returning with my hair
After my great transgression - so requite
Favour renewed, and add a greater sin
By prostituting holy things to idols
....

he has the fact of derivation in mind. The consecrated strength, 'The favour renewed' are holy things because they derive from God.

When he exhorts:
Be of good courage; I begin to feel
Some rousing motions in me..........

he is certain that the 'rousing motions' derive from God. This explains his calm confidence. The great choric invocation:

Go, and the Holy One
Of Israel be thy guide
........that Spirit that first rushed on thee
In the camp of Dan,
Be efficacious in thee now at need!

For never was from Heaven imparted
Measure of strength so great to mortal seed
As in thy wondrous actions hath been seen

is an invocation of that power whence Samson derives his strength.

The final consolation derived by Manoa is that Samson has accomplished his life's mission with God standing by him.

....

And, which is best and happiest yet, all this
With God not parted from him, as was feared,
But favouring and assisting to the end.

The poem ends on a resounding affirmation of God imparting his mystery to his elect, testing and trying him, and then justifying and glorifying him. Referring to this concept, Hutchinson observes:

"The idea of God's calling or election of some men was not unpalatable to Milton. He never questioned that he was himself among the elect, chosen of God to a lofty destiny. Whether we approve the doctrine or not, we cannot fail to see that this side of the Calvinistic creed was a very powerful incentive in the life of the typical puritan, of Cromwell no less than of Milton. To believe that he is destined and called to fulfil the purpose of God, and that he is assured of divine grace to uphold him in his life and of salvation hereafter is enough to give a man courage and inflexible resolution; he can face opposition and obloquy and apparent failure with faith unshaken. That is the real strength of the Calvinistic faith and it is illustrated in the lives and characters of the best Puritans, not least in Milton himself".[19]

"That this concept had gained the full assent of his being is shown by the fact in 1654 he was convinced that Cromwell was the favoured object of the divine regard, elevated by the special direction of the Deity to the highest pinnacle of power".[20]

An important corollary of Samson being God's elect is that the role of the chorus is significantly affected. Being God's elect means in certain ways to be above the rest of humanity in knowledge and wisdom. And even if in a stricken state such a man's knowledge and wisdom may not longer be of that original, seminal nature, his having been called by God *ipso facto* cannot but set him apart from the rest of men. This is not like saying that a king or a queen in a play is set apart from the rest of the characters. The king is certainly at the summit of the hierarchy in not recognising the worth and relevance of what Samson was seeking to accomplish through his marriages and superhuman deeds.

One important function assigned to the chorus is to represent the eyes for the blind Samson, to introduce the various personages that appear at intervals to meet Samson, to describe them and thereupon elicit his reaction whether instant or gradual. In this capacity, the chorus is the means of interpreting the character of the protagonist, of clarifying the essentials of his nature through the encounters that ensue.

But while the chorus is doing all that, it is denied that measure of athleticism and self-assuredness which would seem to distinguish the Greek chorus which knows how to flaunt itself in the midst of a dialogue with a felt spirit of justice and independence. As already illustrated, in the face of grave wrongs being done, of an unjust course of action, or of an affront to honour and dignity, the chorus in Sophocles or Aeschylus or Euripides seldom knows how to hold its tongue.

Quite unlike the usual practice of the Greek dramatists, Milton restricts the scope of the choral action to the extent that he does not allow them to address themselves meaningfully to any of Samson's visitors. The only exception is when the chorus talks to Manoa who has come entertaining a deceptive hope after Samson has left for the temple of Dagon.

Obviously, the chorus has not been allowed to develop that confidence in itself which alone would have enabled it to deliver a well-merited snub to either Dalila or Harapha. And the reason for that lack of self-confidence would seem to be that the chorus is near - completely overshadowed by Milton's protagonist. A sort of alter-ago of Samson, the chorus is nearly swallowed up and outstripped by the much superior presence of God's elect, whereupon it would seem to curl itself deferentially, becoming almost an appendage of the hero. Far from displaying anything of the buoyant autonomy of the Greek chorus, it is content to be near-frozen into the relative inconsequentiality of its position.

We shall discuss two other aspects of *Samson Agonistes* to show further how the essential spirit of the work is Biblical or, say, more Biblical than Greek. These aspects refer to the treatment of the Philistian pride and the misogynic utterance of the chorus.

On Milton's treatment of the Philistines, the following comment is worth noting.

"The principle of hybris is invoked................in the description of the Philistines, and a final chorus applies to them precisely the formula of the Greeks. Offended at their mad pride, God sends to them a spirit of frenzy - the ancient Ate who impairs their judgements and makes them bring on themselves, by their own acts, an avenging Nemesis".[23]

shows, apart from providing information to the audience, that the chorus commands respectful attention, that the queen feels obliged to satisfy its doubts. The Argive elders are no underlings, they stand and move, ask and demand in their own right.

In *Promethus Bound* the chorus finds occasion to reprove Prometheus in the presence of Hermes.

> Hermes seems to us
> to speak not altogether out of season.
> He bids you leave your obstinacy and seek
> a wise good counsel. Hearken to him.
> Shame
> It were for one so wise to fall in error.[21]

On the other hand, it is the same chorus who, when sought to be frightened away by Hermes, looks him straight in the face and answers:

> Say some thing else
> different from this: give me some other counsel
> that I will listen to: this word of yours
> for all its instancy is not for us.
> How dare you bid us practice baseness? We
> will bear along with him what we must bear.[22]

It is obvious, then, that the chorus edges in significant, even tart, comments in the course of a dialogue between important characters. Showing a deep sense of involvement, it does not hesitate to spring to the defence of the oppressed, or to point out, not always to curry favour but sometimes at considerable risk of being reproved, merit and substance in the arguments adduced by the other side. It does not shrink away from conversation with characters other than the hero or the heroine. In fact, whenever it is opportune or appropriate, the chorus addresses them even as it is addressed by them.

By contrast, the sympathetic chorus in *Samson Agonistes* does not even once come anywhere near snapping at either Dalila or Harapha or the officer when they are having a testy and lengthy debate with Samson. In fact, one can see more than one moment when the rapier-thrust of an indignant comment was called for. The chorus provides, aside from some glimpses of Samson's past, the social and religious background against which the action of the play must be sought to be understood. It expresses a fierce and jealously guarded faith in God's special dispensation to the Israelites and it comments on the obtuseness of society but the rest of those making up the hierarchy have their station and rank duly allotted to them. They have their rights and privileges deriving from the constitution of the polity even as the king has his. the king must acknowledge some obligations to those below and cannot take away the citizens' rights and treat them in a way that does not seem to give them their due. At least in the Greek view of things, the ruler has nothing extra-ordinary about him, nothing extra-terrestrial. He must uphold justice and any presumption on his part will be answered by divine wrath. In a word, he is himself held in the framework of law as others are. Which explains the pronounced note of independence that characterises the utterances of the dramatis personae in Greek tragedy. Everyone asserts himself within his sphere and everyone is jealous of his rights with no encroachment expected. And when there is a sign of encroachment or curtailment of rights, they will not shrink from calling a spade a spade. This spirit of freedom and independence generally informs the dialogues, especially the choric utterances which are self-assured and fearless.

Here is a dialogue between Clytemnestra and the chorus from *Agamemnon:*

Chorus - What have you said? Your words escaped my unbelief.
Clyt - The Achaeans are in Troy. Is that not clear enough?
Chorus - This slow delight steals over me to bring forth tears.
Clyt - Yes, for your eyes betray thecloyal heart within.
Chorus - Yet, how can I be certain? Is there some evidence?
Clyt - There is, then must be; unless a God has lied to me.
Chorus - Is it dream visions, easy to believe, you credit?
Clyt - I accept nothing form a brain that is dull with sleep.
Chorus - The charm, then, of some rumour, that made rich your hope?
Clyt - Am I some young girl, that you find my though is so silly?
Chorus - How long, then, is it since the citadel was stormed?
Clyt - It is the night, the mother of this dawn I harked.
Chorus - What kind of messenger could come in speed like this?

Clytemnestra is indeed very much the queen. But what is noteworthy for our purpose is that the chorus talks to her as man to man. It is self-assured and dignified; it does not shrink from questinoning, its object is to get at the truth and not to take anything but the truth, no matter whether the queen is vexed and her patience is taxed in the process. The answer to the last question quoted above comes in an elaborate form which

This, then, is Jehova's way with his idolatrous detractors - making them increasingly contumacious and insensate in their folly, that is, striking them with 'blindness internal'.

One may further recall the confusion of Egypt that is related later. Jehova says:

"And the spirit of Egypt shall fall in the midst thereof; and I will destroy the counsel thereof: and they shall seek to the idols, and to the charmers..............................and to the wizards."

(Isaiah 19:3)

A little later:

'The Lord hath mingled a perverse spirit in the midst thereof: and they have caused Egypt to err in every work thereof, as a drunken man staggereth in his vomit.

(Ibid. 19:14)

Thus the idea of God sending a 'perverse spirit' to rob the wicked of their sense can be more immediately traced to the Old Testament and the spirit attributed by the Semichorus to 'our living Dread' need not, therefore, be emplained with reference to 'Ate', especially when Milton is explicitly talking about the Hebrew God in a clearly defined religious context. The fact that *Samson Agonistes* has the form and structure of Greek tragedy with it chorus, messenger and stichomythia and its unities cannot perhaps alter the other fact that the underlying spirit of the work is that of the Old Testament.

As for the choric denunciation of women in *Samson Agonistes,* much has been made of what may be called the Euripidean influence on Milton. In *Hippolytus,* the protagonist, vowed to celibacy as a worshipper of Artemis, delivers a blistering attack on women in general directly he learns of his stepmother Phaedra having conceived an illicit passion for him.

Women! This coin which men find counterfeit?
Why, why, Lord Zeus, did you put them in the world,
in the light of the sun? If you were so determined
to breed the race of man, the source of it
should not have been women.

....

....

But now, to bring this plague into our homes
we drain the fortunes of our homes.
In this
we have a proof how great a curse is woman
....24

The Scriptural notion of God is of one of an exceptional severity of temper smiting down sooner or later all manner of iniquity, all attempts at affront, disparagement and calumny.

"I the Lord thy God *am* a jealous God, visiting the iniquity of the fathers upon the children into the third and fourth generations of them that hate me".

(Exodus 20:5)

The jealous God cannot bear with the Philistine presumption any longer. It is important to note that Samson had already put this very thought to Manoa in a language most suggestively looking forward to the great event that rounds off the play.

All the contest is now
'Twixt God and Dagon. Dagon hath presumed
Me overthrown, to enter lists with God,
His deity comparing and preferring
Before the God of Abraham; He, be sure,
Will not connive, or linger, *thus provoked*
But *will arise, and his great name assert.*
Dagon must stoop, and *shall ere long receive*
Such a discomfit as shall quite despoil him
Of *all those boasted trophies won on me,*
And *with confusion blank his worshippers.*

(italics added)

Here is a prophetic prevision of a jealous God's work, in acquitting his servant and punishing his enemies at the moment of their triumph and self-adulation. It is not unheard of that this God has set the impious and wicked stubbornly on the wrong track, has caused in them suicidal folly in order to drive them on to their ruin. One recalls the way Jehova dealt with Pharaoh.

"For Pharaoh will say of the children of Israel, They are entangled in the land, the wilderness hath shut them in.

"And I will harden Pharaoh's heart that he shall follow after them; and I will be honoured upon Pharaoh and upon his host; that the Egyptians may know that I am the Lord..

"And I, behold, I will harden the hearts of the Egyptians, and they shall follow them: and I will get the honour upon Pharaoh, and upon all his host, upon his chariots and upon his horsemen".

(Exodus 14:3, 4 & 17)

Without necessarily disputing the interpretation which sees the influence of the Greek conception of Nemesis on Milton's treatment of the Philistines, it may not be entirely unjustifiable to draw attention to another source for an understanding of what Milton is doing here.

Let us turn to the Semichorus celebrating with ringing music the triumph of Samson over his enemies. The Semichorus mentions "a spirit of phrenzy" having been sent among the Philistines "drunk with idolatry, drunk with wine" by "our living Dread, who dwells/In Silo, His bright sanctiary". This spirit "hurt their minds/And urged them on with mad desire/To call in haste for their destroyer". As we have just seen, critics find here the influence of Greek thought. The spirit of frenzy is but hubris which impairs judgement before one's fall and which is the work of 'Ate', the goddess of retribution and revenge. That Milton was greatly influenced by a wide variety of literary and religious ideas is an established fact. What better testimony to the Greek influence is needed than Milton's own foreword to *Samson Agonistes?*

And yet a certain caution may not be out of place when we are trying to get at the spirit of the Semichorus. The hard precision with which the source of emanation of the 'phrenzy' is mentioned is not be mistaken. It is no other then 'our living Dread' who was being sought to be subordinated by the Philistines to their idol, viz, Dagon.

What the chorus is out to do is to emphasise the affront being offered to the true God, the resulting contest between him and Dagon and the final trouncing of the latter. It is the glory of God's triumph that is being sought to be brought into focus. The Hebrew God rendering the infidels' minds deranged, thus paving the way for their destruction reestablishes his superiority that was challenged. Samson had already formulated the issue in his parley with Harapha.

> ....His eye
> Gracious to re-admit the suppliant;
> In confidence whereof I once again
> Defy thee to the trial of mortal fight,
> By combat to decide whose God is God,
> Thine, or whom I with Israel's sons adore.

So the issue is whose God is God? As we listen to the Semichorus the issue has been settled - it is Israel's God that is God.

It is a religious issue - for how can we fail to recognise the fact that for Milton it was not merely a question of demonstrating the true worth of Israel's God as contrasted with hollow vaunt (reminiscent of Harapha's) of Dagon but also of being true to the traditional conception, or rather the scriptural image of this God?

In *Samson Agonistes*, as the treacherous Dalila takes leave of Samson, thwarted in her mission, the chorus, taking its cue from the protagonist, launches an equally bitter attack on women.

It is not virtue, wisdom, valour, wit,
Strength, comeliness of shape, or amplest merit
That woman's love can win or long inherit;
....
Is it that such outward ornament
Was lavished on their sex, that inward gift,
Were left for haste unfinished, judgement scant,
....
Once jointed, the contrary she proves, a thorn
Intestine, far within defensive arms
A cleaving mischief ....

In spite of the apparent similarity of tone, the two utterencesneed to be appraised in their proper context.

Phaedra is helpless in her passion for Hippolytus but as yet she means no harm to him. Arguably, the nurse has been inapt in intimating it to Hippolytus, who is a votary of Artemis, the virgin-goddess and who combines dislike of sex with admiration for beauty. But his being so does not quite justify the acerbity and violence of his attack on women in general - an attack which is devoid of reason and decorum and, in the bargain, an open affront to Aphrodite. His intemperate utterance betokens pride (hubris) and Nemesis is at hand. Ate is at work.

Curiously, in *Samson Agonistes* the attack on women issues not from Samson (whose marital experiences would be somewhat of a justification for such a course) but from the chorus. Even when he is hard on Dalila who, he knows, has come to lure him again into a trap, Samson is unsparing in censuring himself. It is not Dalila but he himself, as he affirms with haunting iteration, who is the cause of his fall, of 'Heaven's desertion'. As Dalila takes leave, at once self-righteous and crest-fallen, Samson's anger falls more heavily down on himself than on her.It is his frailty, his folly which is the focus of judgement.

'God sent her to debase me,
Aggravate my folly ....'

It is important to note how discriminating Milton is in providing the perspective. For the fallen Samson who is nevertheless hopeful of God's pardon, the focal point is his own folly which needs expiation. For the chorus which has, unfortunately, not given much evidence of a sensitive existence during Samson's exchanges with Manoa and Dalila, what continues to be of over-riding importance is female infidelity. It would appear as though the chorus has at long last decided to say something really impressive for the occasion. On Dalila's departure, they refer to her as 'serpent', a view which is endorsed by Samson who himself refers to her as a 'viper'. But the chorus's next speech delivered with a superior tone falls wide of the mark. The choral insinuation that Samson must have had some remnant left of his passion for Dalila is hotly repudiated by him. Whereupon, not unlike a person who is suddenly stung into awareness that it is not yet too late to mend matters, the chorus impetuously launches upon a stinging attack on women - an attack which Samson himself perhaps may not be approving of in its entirety and which incidentally points no less the folly of Samson than the undependability of women. It may be observed that what the chorus does is to seize upon and generalise in sweeping terms the thought that Samson had himself expressed in one of his ripostes to Dalila:

> 'That wisest and best men, full oft beguiled,
> With goodness pricipled not to reject
> The prenitent, but ever to forgive,
> are drawn to wear out miserable days,
> Entangled with a poisonous bosom-snake,
> If not by quick destruction soon cut off,
> As I by thee, to ages an example.'

Samson speaks on the spur of the moment and the tenor of his speech has its appropriateness in its own context.

Now, the chorus in denouncing women in terms rather unexpected of it, not only outdoes Samson but would seem to imply, if unwittingly, criticism of Samson's own conduct.

> What pilot so expert but need must wreck,
> Exbarked with such a steers-mate at the helm?
>
> ....
>
> Therefore God's universal law
> Gave to the man despotic power
> Over the female in due awe,
> Not from that right to part an hour,
> Smile she or lour..........................

Going by the way the position is set forth, Samson is at fault too, for, by her very definition the woman will work for disaster, but the man should take advantage of God's exhortation to Eve which is explicit: 'thy desire shall be to thy husband, and he shall rule over thee'.

(Genesis 3:16)

Samson was remiss in not acting under that law and therefore came to grief. The choric ode thus cuts both ways.

One is accordingly driven to the conclusion that the two misogynic passages in Milton and Euripides are not on all fours. The choral utterance is no unmitigated misogyny as Hippolytus's is, as it envisages exceptions where the wife can be a boon.

'Happy that house....................................'

Besides, even within the general framework where the wife is likely to prove unreliable and treacherous, there does exist an insurance for the man if he has the good sense of governing his home under 'God's univeral law'.

It is the Biblical (the Old Testament) view-point, which, though given an unpleasantly strident expression, holds back from dubbing woman an unqualified and absolute disaster and excluding all chances for man's happiness. The Euripidean lambast, as put in the mouth of Hippolytus, is unqualified misogyny.

Thus whether we think of the conception of the hero, the role of the chorus or the general view of woman in relation to man, Milton's mind works in its distinctive way. It should not be difficult to see then how misleading it would be to try to understand the ruling pre-occupations of *Samson Agonistes* entirely in terms of the Greek tragic temper.

References

1. *A Milton Handbook,* J. H. Hanford & J.C. Traffe (Prentice-Hall.Inc.) 1970,p236.
2, 'Tragic Effect in Samson Agonistes' in Milton, *Modern Eassays in Criticism,* ed. A.E. Barker, O.U.P. 1965, p 447.
3. *Oedipus the King,* 745 & 828 -29 in *Greek Tragedies. Vol I. ed. David Grene and Richmond Lattimore, the University of Chicago Press.*
4. *Oedipus at Colonus,* 962 et. seq. in *Greek Tragedies*-Vol.,3 ed. Grene & Lattimore. The University of Chicago Press.
5. *Promethous Bound,* 244 et. seq, *Greek Tragedies.* Vol. I.
6. Ibid., 1090 et. seq.
7. *Philoctetes,* 446 et. seq, *Greek Tragedies.* Vol. 3.
8. *Hippolytus,* 1380-81, in *Greek Tragedies.* Vol. 1.
9. *Oedipus al Colonous,* 964-65 in *Greek Tragedies.* Vol. 3.

10. '*Paradise Regained* and *Samson Agonistes*' in *Milton Criticism - Selections from Four Centuries*, ed. J. Thorpe, 1965, p 247.
11. *Form and Meaning in Drama*, University, Paperbacks. Methuen, 1960, p 238.
12. Ibid, p 236
13. Romans 8 : 28-30
14. P.L. Bk. III
15. P.L. Bk. III
16. P.L. Bk. VI
17. 'The Sublime Art- Notes on Milton and Holderlin in the *Living Milton*, ed. Frank kermode, 1967,p 153.
18. 'An Introduction to Milton's Poems' in *Milton Criticism - Selections from Four Centuries*, ed. J.Thorpe, 1965, p 259.
19. *Milton and the English Mind*, 1960, pp 174-175.
20. Milton's Prose Works, Bohn, p 290.
21. *Prometheus Bound* 1035 et. seq. in *Greek Tragedies*, Vol. I.
22. Ibid 1063 et. seq.
23. *A Milton handbook*, J.H. Handford and J.C. Taaffe, p 237.
24. Hippolytus, 616 et. seq, *Greek Tragedies* - Vol. i.

HAMLET AND SAMSON AGONISTES

"I tell you, captain, if you look in the maps of the 'world, I warrant you shall find, in the comparisons between Macedon and Monmouth that the situations, look you, is both alike. There is a river in Macedon; and there is also moreover a river at Monmouth: it is called Wye at Monmouth; but is out of my prains what is the name of the other river; but 'tis all one, 'tis alike as my fingers, and there is salmons in both. If you mark Alexander's life well, Harry of Monmouth's life is come after it indifferent well; for there is figures in all things".

(Henry V, IV, VII)

Approaching works of art one cannot be too sure that one is not seeing points of similarity as Fluellen does in the above passage. There is all the neeed for being on one's guard in attempting comparisons, for the danger of landing up in absurd banalities is all too real. The absurdly external parallelism that recommends itself to Fluellen is totally absent when one looks at *Hamlet* and *Samson Agonistes*. They are almost antipodal and belong to two different worlds, as it were. The differences are so sharp and decisive as to call for a dismissal of any attempt at seeing any points that there might be in common. However, it might not be altogether pointless or unrewarding trying to see and pinpoint some remakably like configurations lying concealed beneath the stark dissimilarities between these two remarkable works of art. We hope we will not be concerned with 'gay comparisons' such as Antony dismisses indignantly in favour of what he considers a juster comparison between himself and Caesar (*Antony and Cleopatra* III. xiii). Let us begin with the differences.

Hamlet presents a world which is substantially cut off from the anchorage of medieval thought and which is like a ship whose captaincy has been usurped through foul treachery and which is inwardly rotting, though only in the eyes of the discerning. God is further away than he ever was from man's thought in the earlier age. The certainty of a living faith and the secure clarity of vision have disappeared in the unceratainty and disquiet of a scarcely perceived providence. It is a bedimmed world where the rule of reason which ensures moral and spiritual health in the life of the community and the individual has been undermined almost beyond correction and recovery.

It is a pronouncedly secular world in which the hero, the victim of appalling circumstances, was once the model of a soldier, a scholar, a courtier-a man of the world with singular worldly accomplishments. Even when in the grip of an unsettling trauma as he is now, he gives convincing evidence of what must have been, in the earlier days of normality, a keen, fullblooded participation in the varied affairs of life, remaining equally at home in the world of 'emperor and clown', of men of all stations. Hamlet is at home with the soldier, with the player, the grave-digger, with the courtier. He is, or let us say was, a lover. He is a scholar, a thinker, a poet. He is equal to any situation, whether of his own making (witness 'the play within the play' scene) or of some one else's. A master of rhetoric, of quibbling, of poetry, of mind-boggling thought, he is versatile, answering to the versatility of interests such as only the Renaissance knew.

The play involves the tragic and the comic, the sublime and the profane, the beautiful and the macabre. It involves the crudest melodrama and human thought at its intensest and most rarefied and breath-taking. The hero contemplates the paradox that is man and is himself a paradox. He is at once impulsive, wilful, ratiocinative and profound. In spite of the fixation that haunts him and bedevils his proceeding, such is the variety and amplitude of his mind that he finds himself responding with obvious zest to every happening around him. His psychic agony does not diminish his vitality in any significant manner. He is no statue-like jilted lover or petrified son of an incestuous mother.

The play is a world which, apart from the main throughfare, is full of lanes and by-lanes suggesting the excitedly varied interests and the complex fuleness of life the Renaissance epitomised. Its scope connects earth and heaven and hell, but is not set in one exclusive framework. Both pagan and Christain elements connect. Such is the manipulation of the situational potential and the psychological thrust that characters are kept painfully guessing at the true import of situations. This results in the provocative mysteriousness that is the keynote of a milieu which imprisons man as though in a mist and which in the process of dramatisation brings out tellingly what Keats saw as Shakespeare's supreme gift, viz, the negative capability - the power to remain in a state of uncertainty, doubt and anxiety "without any irritable reaching after fact and reason." The dramatist's prickly awareness of many-layered and contradictory experiences and his tense resolution to spread out, to probe and to variegate appeal at the popular and sophisticated levels easily distinguish this play from the less bustling and more exclusively focussed drama of the ancients and of Milton.

Milton's *Samson Agonistes*, very much like his *Paradise Lost*, is set within the medieval framework of god-man relationship. It suggests the certainty of God and the medieval sense of man's nearness to God. The lapsed man's eclipsed sense of the immediacy of God's presence is only an ironic device used to dramatise the living reality of God being where He is not suspected to be and being ever mindful of his devotee or champion. Samson is God- intoxicated, and in that sense a mono-maniac and whatever concern he has for his nation is prompted by his sense of accountability to God. Indeed, Milton is out to justfiy the ways of God to man. His hero does not recognise anything as of value unless it has an explicit relevance to his mission as God's champion on earth. This explains the character of the work and the method that Milton adopts to realise his aim. Much of what Shakespeare needs is superfluous or almost blasphemous to him. He needs only a handful of characters, a scrupulously narrowed arena, and he will keep to the thoroughfare, being contemptuous of lanes and by-lanes which can only provide criminal diversion from the urgent need to arrive and vindicate. He has no use for an appeal at the popular level, for unlike in Shakespeare, people, by and large, are a contemptible quantity. The Renaissance multiplicity of human concerns gives way to the exclusive concern of man seeking his God, for this seeking is what matters to the exclusion of everything else. And whenever God and the world are mentioned in the same breath, the former takes precedence over the latter.

What is in question in *Hamlet* is the status of man and the credibility of reason as of potency enough to sustain man's superiority over the animal world, while what is of obsessive interest in *Samson Agonistes* is man's accountability to his maker, The nature of vidication at the end of Milton's work sets off, as nothing else could so tellingly, Hamlet's sense of being cut off prematurely. He has lamentably not been allowed the time to render a true account of all that has gone before, so that his people remain 'unsatisfied'. For him death marks no triumph. The 'fell sergeant' has denied him the time he needed ('Had I but time'). Still another point is that the world of *Samson Agonistes* is remarkably incident-free except at the end, unlike that of Hamlet which is packed with a variety of incidents. The closed world of the court is counterpointed by a whole bustle of life.

Such differences as we have noted above are likely to preclude any scope for a worth-while comparative study involving perceptions of kinship in one respect or another. Nevertheless one can see some striking similarities in outline and detail between *Samson Agonistes* and *Hamlet*, and the resemblances strike one as all the more revealing on account of the over-all divergencies in conception and execution.

Samson is literally in enemy territory and in prison. Hamlet is virtually in enemy territory and in prison. Claudius talks of Hamlet's'transformation', but thanks to the appalling transformation brought about by fratricide Hamlet finds himself an alien in his own land and talks of being in prison.

There was a divine secret imparted to Samson, who having divulged it in a weak, unguarded moment, now bewails his apostasy. To Hamlet, too, a dread secret has been entrusted, but, unlike Samson, he has kept the sanctity of it. Hamlet's present predicament is due to an act of treachery on the part of his uncle and infidelity on the part of his mother coupled with obtuseness on the part of Ophelia. In a manner not entirely dissimilar, Samson's bondage and his blinded state have been brought about by treachery on the part of his own people, especially Dalilah.

Samson's, wife acts as a tool in the hands of his enemy, so that he stands alienated and betrayed. Hamlet's mother has gone over to the usurper, being guilty of marital apostasy, while his erstwhile friends have become tools of his enemy.

Both Hamlet and Samson condemn the untrustworthy character of women as a class. Hamlet's fury and sarcasm in the nunnery and closet scenes bear a striking family resemblance to Samson's explosive denunciation of women in his encounter with Dalilah. The cynicism epitomised in the formulation 'frailty.thy name is woman' is not far removed in temper from Samson's vitriolic denunciation of woman as a 'poisonous bosom-snake'.

The fortunes of both protagonists touch the nadir of despair and both resort to selflaceration, the discrepant nature of the causes not withstanding. A feeling of inadequacy, of not being equal to the occasion demoralises both for a while. Samson is borne down by a sense of the inscrutablility of God's ways, Hamlet by a sense of the sphinx-like mystery of life and death. Both reflect mournfully on the paradox that is man - how he is at once the glory and the shame of creation. Both lament the enslavement of reason by passion. And in both the plays crippling doubt eventually gives way to rejuvenating faith. While this statement might seem too strong and categorical to be applied to the Hamlet world, the fact remains that what had seemed difficult, almost impossible of attainment comes withing easy reach when the muddy stream of scepticism merges in the rising tide of belief. The thread that snapped is joined again. The 'exiled' man is restored. (This restoration is peculiarly valid for Samson, while for Hamlet it can only be construed as a sudden upswing stopping short of yielding complete fulfilment. He has a sense of being snatched away before time. The vision of man at odds with the existential situation abides. The word remains till the end 'out of joint'. The restoration we are talking of is of ephemeral effect almost like that of a mirage).

Inspite of the caveat thus entered for Hamlet, it will be noticed that Hamelt and Samson both get their revenge with a measure of unexpectedness, the accomplishment of the task (however unsatisfactory for Hamlet) being rather slow to come. In either case, there are two phases. In the first phase, i.e., the phase of alienation and sterility, the protagonist is groping, questioning and whiplashing himself in enveloping darkness. In the second phase, i.e., the phase of recovery, he has reached the healing waters of faith, leaving sterility behind. For both the process is one of graduation from a state of spiritual crisis. Both Shakespeare and Milton dramatise the growth of the soul, its upward swing. Paradoxically, there could be nothing more unexpected than Hamlet's resound-let's resounding claim in the final scene:

> There's a divinity that shapes our ends,
> Rough-hew them how we will.
>
> (V.ii 10-11)

He is settled in mind and will respond to the King's summons, even when Horatio counsels caution. Not dissimilar is Samson's sudden thrust of mind:

> I begin to feel
> Some rousing motions in me, which dispose
> To something extraordinary my thoughts.

Samson's 'presage' (If there be aught of presage in the mind') echoes Hamlet's 'augury' ('Not a whit, we defy augury: there's special providence in the fall of a sparrow.)

These miracles of utterances acquire their electrifying effect, their sustance, indeed their authenticity from the enormity of the suffering borne and the resulting growth of the soul.

"The soldier on guard who cannot leave his post until he is relieved or given permission from above, is a metaphor for the soul in this world which comes very easily to Renaissance writers".[1] The conception is of a sentinel ever awake and watchful, holding to his appointed station without a thought of yielding to the foe. Both Hamlet and Samson are such sentinels and they are conceived remarkably alike. Whereas Hamlet proves true to the conception in holding his fort (the privacy of his soul and the dourness of his vision of man), defeating all attempts at despoiling him of his secrets and making inroads on his preserves, Samson proves guilty of a criminal slackening of vigilance, resulting in the enemy lapping up his 'secret', and in his impotence and present ignominy. Hence, the unremitting self-chastisement and hence, in Dalila's words 'the eternal tempest never to be calmed'.

In characteristic Renaissance imagery, Milton represents his protagonist's failure to be worthy of his charge.

> How could I once look up, or heave the head
> *Who like a foolish pilot, have ship-wracked*
> *My vessel* trusted to me from above
> Gloriously rigged, and for a word, a tear,
> Fool! have divulged the secret gift of God
> To a deceitful woman?
>
> (italics added)

Again, changing the image, yet retaining the suggestion:

> What boots it at one *gate* to make *defence*,
> And *at another let in the foe*,
> Effeminately vanguished?
>
> (italics added)

The soldier-image of Hamlet which must have been a conscious part of the over-all dramatic conception comes through fluently and convincingly in Fortinbras's speech at the end:

> Let four captains
> Bear Hamlet like a *soldier* to the stage;
> For he was lilkey, had he been put on,
> To have prov'd most royal; and for his passage,
> The *soldier's* music and the rite of war
> Speak loudly for him.
>
> (italics added)
> (V.ii.388 et.seq)

Even when Hamlet proves invulnerable as a soldier at his post, he fights constantly under the threat of a siege. He can see the evil masquerading as virtue while 'rank corruption mining all within/Infects unseen?

The conception of a soldier given a solemn charge is reinforced by the following description given by Manoa of a rejuvenated Samson as he visualises the situation:

> And I persuade me God hath not permitted
> His strength to grow up with his hair
> *Garrisoned round about him like a camp*
> *Of youthful soldiery*............ (Italics added)

The overwhelming feeling of the ubiquity and decisiveness of defilment is germane to the visions worked out in the two works. Both protagonists are victims of an unclean regime. Samson's feeling of being tainted and unclean is all too palpable and he has the additional feeling of having brought it upon himself through sinning. While Hamlet is innocent of any such offence as Samson accuses himself of, he is not free either from the sense of guilt. As he reflects on the situation, he unavoidably has a share of the corruption that has gone too deep into the human stock ('virtue cannot so inoculate our old stock but we shall relish of it'). 'With more offences at my beck than I have thoughts to put them in', Hamlet too feels tainted and sick. Hecalls himself an 'arrant knave'.

Conceived as God's champion, Samson eventually turns our to be the cleanser that he was destined to be. What about Hamlet? One notices an atavistic tendency that Shakespeare implants in his hero. Could it be that in his awe-skuck allusion to Hercules in his first soliloquy ('but no more like my father/Than I to Hercules'), he was, however unconsciously, glancing at the cleanser-image of that mythical hero? Could it be that Shakespeare made him recognise, however dimly, a compulsive, if intimidating intimation from the conjuration of that puissant pagan image? In other words, could it be that Shakespeare had all but cast him in that role only to see how in his vision of the dismembered time, such a role would turn out to be? Hamlet's habitual language with reference to the corruption of the time is of one who looks upon himself as a possible cleanser, purifier. Habitually, he thinks of and harps on the general corruption, the rotting of the state rather than the single act of teacherous murder which could be more of a symptom than the cause of the ever-spreading malady. He generalises the evil and its destructive character so that the world is "an unweeded garden,/That grows to seed; things rank and gross in nuture/Possess it merely".The often-noticed generalising bent of Hamlet goes well with, in fact, gives point to, his projected role of redeemer, however dismayed in spirit he may feel contemplating his task:

The time is our of joint. O cursed spite,
That ever I was born to set it right !

(1.v. 189-90)

In the last act Hamlet asks Horatio if it is "not to be damn'd/To let this canker of our nature come/In further evil'. He is thinking with revulsion and horror of the further harm that might issue from Claudius and he is thinking not merely of the murder of his father, but also of the staining of his mother. of being deprived of his claim to the throne and of the treacherous design on his life. His concern is how "not to be damn'd" and how to extirpate this spreading evil.

The debasement of the situation brought about by sin is focused on in both works by a similarity of means. Both Shakespeare and Milton make use of divine imagery, of the contrast between a greater and a lesser divinity to emphasise the almost immeasurable gulf between the present and the past, between what was and what is, between the radiance that was and its monstrous eclipse. Hamlet refers to the past splendour and the present monstrosity in terms of Hyperion and Satyr:

But two months dead! Nay, not so much, not two.
So excellent a king that was to this
Hyperion to a Satyr;

(1.ii. 138 et seq)

In the closet scene, he speaks to his mother:

Look here upon this picture and on this.
See what a grace was seated on this brow;
Hyperion's curls; ....
Look you now what follows
Here is your husband, like a mildew'd ear
Blasting his wholesome brother

(III.iv. 53 et seq)

Hyperion-Satyr antithesis symbolises the Renaissance antithesis of reason and passion; the triumph of Satyr over Hyperion signifies the displacement of reason and the usurpation of its rightful place by passion standing for inordinate amibition, greed, lechery. The insurrection within man overthrowing the rational soul and thus overturning the hierarchy of elements has unleashed the reign of evil. In Hamlet the earlier period is spoken of in terms such as 'fair and war-like', 'majesty' and 'dignity', 'hallowed and gracious', 'our valiant Hamlet'. Hamlet's loving and wistful reference to his dead father ('He was a man, take him for all in all, I shall not look upon his like again') is an anguished tribute to a reign of reason never to return. The present dispensation is that of an 'incestuous and adulterate beast'.

Milton, likewise, drives home Samson's unforeseen subjection to the present abomination in terms of the eclipse of Israel's God and ascendence of Dagon, the abhored Philistine God. The present dispensation is a witness to Dagon reigning in 'pomp' and to 'dishonour' and 'obloquy' brought to Israel's God.

> All the contest is now
> Twixt God and Dagon. Dagon hath presumed,
> Me overthrown, to enter lists with God,
> His deity comparing and preferring
> Before the God of Abraham.

The present regime 'drunk with idolatry, drunk with wine' is an abomination not unlike the one presided over by the Satyr-King, Claudius.

The glory that characteristed the rule of Israel's God is represented by Samson when he was in full possession of reason and in full consciousness of that power which was transmitted to him from above. And the rise of Dagon is accounted for by Samson letting himself be ruled by passion that made a captive of reason.

Shakespeare and Milton dwell upon conjugal infidelity and stress the deification of lust and treachery as the cause and accompaniment of the reign respectively of Satyr and Dagon. The protagonists are trapped and menaced. The feeling of being encircled and thus imperilled expresses itself in a language that is significantly similar, Hamlet talks of being 'benetted round with villainies'. And Samson wails:

> Ye see, o friends,
> How many evils have enclosed me round ....

Both undergo the tortures of the damned. Both are hard upon themselves for being 'lapsed' souls, though for different reasons. Hamlet sees himself as one 'lapsed in time and passion' for having unforgivably put off 'the important acting of thy dread command', while Samson feels 'bereaved', exiled', even 'annulled' for having 'profaned/the mystery of God, given me under pledge/of vow'.

The points of similarity embrace even other aspects. Inspite of the obvious difference in their dramatic roles, Gertrude and Manoa would seem to have a similarity of approach towards the suffering protagonists. Gertrude, not with standing being the cause of Hamlet's crisis of being, continues to love him and would like to see him happy in her own placid way. In fact, it pains her to find her son so unlike his former self, almost transformed beyond recognition-a melacholy, bitter and tortured soul. She wants him to get reconciled to his father's passing as an inevitable happening in a man's life, accept the changed situation and resume his former self when he was the 'observed of all observers', as Ophelia puts it. to be fair to Gertrude, she is unaware of the fact that Claudius has treacherously got her former husband out of his way. On the other hand, epicureanism and lust have rendered her insensitive enough not to realise that her marriage to Claudius so soon after her former husband's death could cause such disquiet in Hamlet's mind. For Hamlet the situation is pestilential.

Not only is Monoa ever ready to ingratiate himself with the Philistine lords to secure Samson's release, he even advises his son to prefer 'self -preservation' to being 'self-rigorous', 'choosing death as due'.

> I already have made way
> To some Philistine lords, with whom to treat
> about thy ransom
>
> ....
>
> Repent the sin; but if the punishment
> Thou canst avoid, self-preservation bids.

Both Gertrude and Monoa symbolise the obtuseness of moral vision. While Monoa represents the spirit of compromise with evil for the sake of worldly comfort and ease, Gertrude is all self-indulgence which, for its uninterrupted proceeding, fears any questioning posture which Hamlet seems to represent. In Gertrude one sees gross, if bland, sensuality asking for approval and acceptance.

In both the plays, then, the parent symbol is a means of spelling out the unbridgeable gulf between the myopia of mundane gratification and a terrifying insistence on being true to the rightful image of man.

Yet in another respect, one can see a nearly indentical thrust. Hamlet's attitude to the two spies,Rosencrantz and Guildenstern, is almost on all fours with Samson's attitude to the 'thirty spies' 'appointed to await me'. Justifying the murder of those spies, Samson says:

> I used hostility, and took their spoil,
> To pay my underminers, in their coin.

Anticipating what he is going to do to the two former school-fellows whom he will trust 'as I will adders fang'd ' because of their being in league with the villainous King, Hamlet chuckles:

> Let it work:
> For 'tis sport to have the engineer
> Hoist with his own petar; and't shall go hard
> But I will delve one yard below their mines
> And blow them at the moon.
>
> (III.iv. 205 et.seq)

Later, justifying his action is sending them to their death in England, Hamlet puts the matter in decisive perspective, using an argument Samson himself might approve of:

> Why, man, they did make love to this employment;
> They are not near my conscience; their defeat
> Does by their own insinuation grow.
>
> (V.ii 57 et.seq)

It is obvious, then, that both Shakespeare and Milton must have apprehended remarkably similar situations though their artistic enactment thereof took on widely different expressions because of their distinctive world-views and the compulsions of their pronouncedly individual talents and temperaments. Indeed, we have already alluded to the basic differences.

At this point we must glance at some other disparities. Both Hamlet and Sasmon are obsessed with death, yet their approaches to it are sharply different. The difference here is a difference between Shakespeare and Milton. The thought of death is natural to a tortured soul. But while Shakespere harbours the idea from time to time, he cannot persist in doing so for long, for death is an insoluble enigma. However painful and unbearable life may be,the thought of death affords no assurance that it will be a better state of affairs when one has wound up the business of life. No such sense of mystery troubles Milton who is fortified by his dogma and his faith. Shakespeare does not seem to know either, at any rate when he is composing his *Hamlet*. He is a tormented and unresting quester. He is an open-eyed questioner subject to the fears natural to a man who would probe the beyond unfettered by prescriptive dogma:

> Who would these fardels bear,
> To grunt and sweat under a weary life,
> But that the dread of something after death

The undiscover'd country, from whose bourn
No traveller returns.

(III. I. 76 et seq)

Contrast this with how Milton's hero longs for death:

This one prayer yet remains, might I be heard,
No long petition; speedy death,
The close of all my miseries and the balm.

Hamlet sees an unknown 'dread' in death, Samson knows no such perplexity. He welcomes death within the religious framework, the framework of faith.

Shakespeare's plays suggest the philosophy of growth. His belief in growth is true not only of the central figures of his plays but also of the minor characters. Gertrude is certainly different at the end of the closet scene. she can be supposed to have felt some stirrings of a moral awakening:

Be thou assur'd, if words be made of breath
And breath of life, I have no life to breathe
What thou hast said to me.

(III.iv. 197 et.seq)

Laertes who has been in league with the king, wakes up at the end of the play to the evil of his proceeding, disowns Claudius, exchanges forgiveness with Hamlet and befriends him. This fact of moral growth is in complete contrast with the staticity of Manoa and Dalila. Manoa's complacency is incorrigible while Dalilah remains self-righteous till the end.

Unlike Milton, Shaekespeare takes us inside his characters. He lets us hear what the chracters think or say to themselves behind the facade of their public selves. Thus we hear Claudius confess, express remorse and ask for God's pardon, although he knows that the retention of the fruits of his crime cannot entitle him to pardon. We hear him praise Hamlet:

..................he, being remiss,
Most generous, and free from all contriving
Will not peruse the foils.

(IV.vii. 134 et seq)

Milton's cast of mind and art are such that he cannot afford us such insights into the character of, say, Harapha or Dalila. We only encounter their public selves.

Claudius's private admiration for Hamlet glances at and is in line with Iago's secret acknowledgement of Othello's goodness and candour: 'The Moor is of a free and open nature' (Othello I III) and Edmund's private view of Edgar:

> ....a brother noble,
> Whose nature is so far from doing harms
> That he suspects none.
>
> (*King Lear* I. ii).

Such utterances constitute an individual trait of Shakespeare's art. They point to and intimate his rounded view of life. And then one cannot but notice his pervasive ambivalence - the multiple perspectives under which the characters and the wide world in which they move are viewed. This ambivalence is reflective of the dramatist's profound recognition of the mystery of life-life that is many-layered and many-faceted and which refuses to be seen against one set perspective. Plurality of vision is the unstated law of the Shakespearean world.

Despite the overtly religious background, Greek drama would seem to be more akin to Shakespearean drama in its focus on and intensification of the basic mystery of life. Both work out in their unique ways the needling awareness of the dimness and ambiguity of human perception and the fatal congruence of fate and character conspiring to weave man's tragic destiny.

And finally, the common, popular touch-an area where Shakespeare is *sui generis*. Milton has no use for the common people 'the common rout,/That wandering loose about,/Grow up and perish as the summer fly,/Heads without name, no more remembered'. And now look at the soldiers who introduce us to the Hamlet world, the players in whose unexpected company Hamlet forgets his melancholy and the grave-diggers whose natural, lusty accent holds Hamlet and reminds us of the elemental character of life and of the inevitability of death—well, it is such characters as they who provide the unique tang and savour of the Shakespearean milieu and create its enthralling ambience.

References:

1. **Helen Gardner,** *The Business of Criticism*, Oxford Paper-backs, 1963,p 49.

INDEX